Pick of the Crop

Pick

of the

Crop

Seasonal Recipes
inspired by Canada's
Public Markets

Jennifer Stamper

Macmillan Canada
Toronto

First published in Canada in 2000 by
Macmillan Canada, an imprint of CDG Books Canada

CANADIAN CATALOGUING IN PUBLICATION DATA

Stamper, Jennifer
    Pick of the crop: seasonal recipes inspired by Canada's public markets

Includes index
ISBN 0-7715-7710-9

1. Cookery, Canadian.   2. Farmer's markets – Canada.   I. Title

TX715.6.S698   2000   641.5971   C00-931182-3

This book is available at special discounts for bulk purchases by your group or organization for sales promotions, premiums, fundraising and seminars. For details, contact: CDG Books Canada Inc., 99 Yorkville Avenue, Suite 400, Toronto, ON, M5R 3K5.

1 2 3 4 5   TRI   04 03 02 01 00

Cover and text design by Counterpunch/Linda Gustafson
All colour photography by John Sherlock, with the exception of Jan's cranberry applesauce cookie by Joe Borelli.
Historical images: City of Ottawa Archives: CA 1478, p. 10; CA 4266, p. 11; Montreal City Archives: p.78; City of Toronto Archives: RG 8-55-16, p. 114; SC 231-613, p. 115
Background photographs on recipe pages by PhotoDisc, Inc and Digital Vision Ltd.
All other black and white photography by Jennifer Stamper, with the exception of the inside cover image supplied by Atwater Public Market, pp. 112 and 119 by Linda Gustafson.

Macmillan Canada
An imprint of CDG Books Canada Inc.
Toronto

Printed in Canada

Dedication

To Grandma Philp, for introducing me to the kitchen, and to my mother, for allowing me unrestricted access, regardless of the mess.

And to my husband, Oliver, sous-chef extraordinaire!

Acknowledgements

This book wouldn't have been possible without the terrific support of my editor, Jill Lambert and the amazing photographic contribution of John Sherlock. I also must thank John Garbutt, assistant market manager for the Byward Market in Ottawa, Patrizia Cusinato, Director of Communications for the Montreal Public Market Management Corporation, and Colleen Welsh, the market manager for Granville Island Public Market. All were generous with their time and effort to provide information regarding market events and history. Most importantly, thank you to all the market vendors, who over the years, have answered many questions and above all, provided high quality local foods.

Contents

Introduction

The idea for a public market cookbook was born out of a love for fresh, seasonal foods and the unique atmosphere that a public market provides. I can remember going to the St. Lawrence Market as a child and coming face to face with a very large octopus tentacle. What an event for a six-year old! Now, as a food stylist living in Vancouver, I frequent Granville Island's Public Market in search of beautiful fruits and vegetables. It is always a wonder to see the market change with the seasons. In the summer, tables are full of local berries and juicy Okanagan peaches. As fall approaches, the colour of the market changes, giving way to mounds of hazelnuts, piles of apples, and heaps of squash.

This transition is true for any public market in Canada. However, the quality and freshness of such local, seasonal foods is often overlooked in favour of foods available year-round at the supermarket. Supermarkets can be convenient, but it's hard to judge the freshness of produce when it's wrapped in plastic; produce that appears fresh can go bad the next day. In order to facilitate transport, fruit destined for supermarkets is picked before it is ripe. This may be acceptable for bananas, which ripen after harvest, but it is disastrous for many other types of fruit. For example, eating an imported strawberry in the middle of winter will never compare to the taste of the juicy berries found at local markets in the late spring and early summer. Berries picked too early simply do not get that extra bit of sunshine needed to develop great strawberry flavour.

Public markets are such lively, social places that they're worth visiting even if you don't plan to buy. Visitors delight in the huge variety of fruits and vegetables, some of which they may have never seen before or have no idea how to use. Of course, the farmers and produce vendors are a great source of information. Although most cookbooks don't have many kohlrabi recipes, the guy who grows this unique-looking vegetable probably has one that's worth a try! Or try striking up a conversation with the local butcher or fishmonger. Ask how the season has been for salmon or what the difference is between organic and free-range beef. Not only will you learn something new about the food you buy but also make your market experience that much more enjoyable.

Besides food, there's lots of other stuff going on at public markets. Street musicians are a popular attraction at all the markets; Granville Island has an informal "stage" outside one entrance, and the sound of a saxophone or violin can often be heard in the front hall of St. Lawrence Market. Local artisans have tables full of pottery, handmade jewelry, and many other interesting crafts. The markets also host seasonal events that are exciting for both tourists and locals alike. At Marché Atwater, locals look forward to the great pumpkin festival where giant pumpkins are carved and kids' faces are painted. In the summer, there's the corn festival at St. Lawrence Market and the tomato festival at Granville Island Market. Ottawa's Byward Market attracts a crowd in the spring, when the stalls are full of flowers.

The recipes that follow are inspired by these wonderful markets and reflect each season's bounty. Although some of the ingredients are available year-round, hearty items, such as kale and beef, seem better suited for the winter table, whereas other ingredients, such as strawberries and asparagus, are classic springtime fare. The recipes highlight these seasonal ingredients and are meant to be simple and satisfying. Use them as a starting point for your cooking inspiration. Enjoy!

Going to Market

Visiting a public market is an exciting event. It's not just about food shopping, it's about experiencing all that the season has to offer and being inspired by it. Here are some tips on how to tackle the huge selection before you.

▼ **First,** check the hours of operation for the market. Weekday and weekend hours can vary, as can the hours for individual shops and stalls. While you're at it, find out about current market events and seasonal festivals.

▼ **Arrive** at the market early. This way you won't have trouble parking and, more importantly, you will be able to walk around freely – enjoying the sights and smells at your own pace. Vendors will also have more time to answer questions since they won't have a lineup to attend to.

▼ **Take** a look around before you start buying. When I arrive at the market I always take an exploratory tour, checking out what looks best. As you look, you may notice that the baby greens look especially perky or that beautiful fresh trout has just been delivered. Guess what you'll be having for dinner?

▼ **Have** enough cash with you. Most vendors do not accept debit or credit cards and, quite often, purchases are only a couple of dollars anyway.

▼ **Buy** lightweight food first, so you don't get weighed down.

▼ **Bring** your own bags for carrying produce. Some of the markets sell cloth bags, which are washable and reusable. This way you don't need individual plastic bags.

▼ **If you** have too many bags to carry, find an empty banana box at one of the produce stands and place your bags in that. Sometimes vendors will let you leave the box with them while you continue shopping. When you're done, you can pick up your box and be on your way.

▼ **Don't forget** to stop for a treat. Have a coffee at the Blue Parrot or a classic peameal bacon sandwich at the Carousel Bakery before you begin shopping on Saturday morning. If it's lunchtime, I usually indulge in an order of fresh-cut french fries with lots of salt and vinegar!

Cooks' Tips

▼ **Spinach** adds colour and nutritional value to soups, stews, curries, and stir-fries. Simply toss a handful of raw leaves into the pot at the end of cooking and let wilt. Stir and serve.

▼ Use a cast iron grill pan for indoor grilling of **steaks** and other meats. Season meat well with salt and pepper for maximum flavour. When grilling meat, turn at equal intervals before blood appears so as not to dry it out. Always let grilled or roasted meat rest at least 5 minutes before carving.

▼ Bake free-form **fruit pies** directly on a preheated pizza stone for a crisp pastry bottom.

▼ Delicate **fresh herbs**, such as basil, taste best when added at the last minute.

▼ **Rosemary** is naturally oily and adds tremendous flavour to soup when it is sautéed with the onions.

▼ **Parmigiano-Reggiano** is worth the money because it has a full, nutty flavour, which goes a long way. Use leftover rinds of Parmegiano-Reggiano to flavour soups. Simply add a small chunk to the soup and let simmer for at least 15 minutes. Dry rinds will keep for months in the refrigerator.

▼ **Crab apples**, baked whole, are wonderful alongside poultry or a pork roast.

▼ Instead of rice, use **couscous** as an accompaniment for a chili or stew. It cooks in about 10 minutes when placed in an equal amount of boiled water or stock. Fluff with a fork and serve.

▼ The acid and sugar in orange juice help to prevent **pastry** becoming tough.

▼ Keep cooked **pasta** from sticking by tossing it with a little olive oil.

▼ When recipes refer to a "pinch" of salt, use the amount you can pinch between your thumb and first two fingers.

Spring
at Byward Market

Established in 1826, Byward Market is one of Canada's oldest and largest public markets. This thriving, four-season market has a rich, colourful history that includes a great fire, class and religious conflict, and the "Stoney Monday Riot." The market once served as a forum for political debate as well as an agricultural and commercial centre. Today, the Byward Market retains much of the flavour of its past. It is Ottawa's central market for seasonal, farm fresh produce and one of the capital's main destinations for both residents and tourists.

Located just down the street from the National Art Gallery, between George and York Streets, the Byward Market is made up of a central market building that is surrounded by tables full of seasonal produce brought in daily by local farmers and producers. In late summer there are stacks and stacks of fragrant strawberries packed in wooden baskets of all sizes and buckets of fresh herbs and flowers. Some of the tables are shaded from the sun by brightly coloured tarpaulins, and a mix of locals and tourists walk around inspecting what the season has to offer. English and French are spoken interchangeably.

For a change of scenery, step inside the old market building and have a fresh bagel, still warm from the wood oven, or a piece of homemade quiche. Check out the various boutiques, and don't miss the display of historical market

photographs located near the main entrance. Use the map of the market to try to place yourself at the site of one of the nineteenth-century images. Just imagine what it would be like to weave your way between the horse-drawn carriages, down unpaved streets, wearing the clothing of the day.

Although the saddlers, tailors, and livestock dealers are gone, the market is still a lively attraction with a unique multicultural history.

Spring

What to Look for at Byward

Spring at Byward Public Market is a season of transition. As the season opens, the air is crisp and the snow is making a steady retreat. Sugarbush farms are open for business and filling the market tables with samples of the year's first batch of maple syrup, maple butter, and maple candies. As the weather warms, evidence of renewal is all around; the market abounds with early spring greens, fiddleheads, herbs, and flowers. Then June arrives and the air is fragrant with the perfume of Ottawa Valley strawberries and bunches of wild garlic. This is the time to peel off the bulky layers of winter clothing and revel in the excitement of a new market season.

Edible Flowers – Byward Public Market is known for its great selection of flowers in the spring. In fact, the entire city is bright with colourful tulips and daffodils. Some flowers are edible and a beautiful addition to a salad of fresh spring greens. Each edible flower has its own flavour; try pansies, violets, dianthus, lavender, geraniums, and marigolds. (Eat only the petals and be sure you purchase only pesticide-free flowers.)

Fresh Herbs – Cooking with fresh herbs is a revelation; once you experience their clear bright flavours you may never go back to using dried herbs again. Fresh herbs are available for purchase year-round now due to specialty greenhouses and some are also easy to grow on a sunny windowsill. Herbs are not only used for seasoning all sorts of foods but also salads with other mixed varieties of greens. This sort of salad mixture leads to bursts of flavour in every bite. Chives are often the first to appear at market. Snip them over food and don't forget the chive flowers, which add colour and taste! Spring thyme is a beautiful grass green in the early months; look for lemon thyme and variegated varieties. Rosemary is young and tender in spring, and the scent of this herb will linger on your hands for hours. Italian or flat-leafed parsley is especially bright at this time of year and indispensable as a garnish.

Asparagus – Spring is the season of asparagus. Not only does it taste fresh and tender at this time but it is also affordable. Early asparagus is usually thin; thicker stalks appear later. One is not better than the other; freshness is what counts. Look for spears with tightly formed heads, brightly coloured stalks, and smooth stems. To prepare asparagus, grab the stalks with both hands and bend them. The asparagus will break at a natural point above which will be the tender part for steaming and grilling and below which, the tough stem, perfect for making an asparagus soup base.

Spinach – In the cooler months of spring, baby spinach gives us a glimpse of summer. Flat-leafed varieties are most often found at the market. Size of the leaf is not an indication of quality; simply look for leaves that are crisp and a deep emerald green. Spinach at its best has a bright, clean flavour whereas spinach past its prime has an unpleasant mineral quality that can be more pronounced when cooked. Spinach is not only a salad green but is wonderful when simply wilted at the last minute into pasta or soup. To wilt spinach, place the washed spinach leaves, still wet, into a pan. Over high heat, turn leaves frequently until just wilted. Drain as required. This technique retains the vibrant colour of the spinach and adds extra nutritional value to any dish.

Peas – Nothing compares to a bowl of squeaky-fresh, English peas. Not much needs to be done with them; a brief plunge into boiling water will bring out their brilliant colour and their sweet taste. After that, a bit of butter and salt and they're ready to eat. At the market, look for medium-sized pea pods with few blemishes. The fatter pea pods, especially the ones where you can see the contour of the peas inside, are more likely to contain older, starchy peas. If you buy your peas from a local producer at the market, you will likely experience the fresh taste that gardeners rave about.

Wild Garlic – If you visit the Byward Market in the spring, look out for wild garlic. Also known as a ramp or wild leek, wild garlic has a stalk like a scallion and tall, tapered leaves. It flourishes especially well in the sugar-maple groves in Canada during the early spring months. Wild garlic has a mild garlic-onion flavour and can be used in much the same way as cultivated garlic, with the bonus that the leaves and bulb are both edible. Choose wild garlic that is bright green with its roots still attached. Store in the refrigerator, tightly wrapped in plastic.

Fiddleheads – A fiddlehead is a young fern that is found throughout the West Coast and as far east as Newfoundland. These "watch-spring" coiled, fern fronds have a flavour much like asparagus or green beans, and are often cooked in the same way. Their whimsical shape makes an attractive addition to any spring vegetable sauteé. Look for tightly curled fiddleheads that are no more than 1½ in. (4 cm) in diameter. Trim the tails (if any), wash well, and use immediately as fiddleheads deteriorate fast.

Morels – Morels are one of the first signs of spring. Harvested from the wild, these little gems are a special treat for mushroom lovers. Morels are cone-shaped, with hollow stems and many small holes on their caps. Choose smaller morels to use whole in sauces and braises and larger ones, chopped, to use in stuffings and soups. Fresh morels should be spongy and dry with a sweet earthy, almost nutty scent. Use within two to three days and store in a brown paper bag in the refrigerator.

Lamb – Spring lamb is succulent. Whether you are roasting a whole leg for Easter or braising some shanks, lamb is a rich indulgence that often marks a special occasion or family gathering. Most people are familiar with a traditional "rack of lamb," but few ever realize the great potential of other relatively inexpensive cuts. Braised lamb shoulder is excellent, as are lamb shanks, which come from the lower leg. When cooked slowly, these cuts develop tremendous flavour and are meltingly tender.

Maple Syrup – What could be more Canadian than maple syrup? Just as North Americans travel to experience true pasta in Italy, Europeans and other visitors seek out the unique flavour of maple syrup. Spring festivals at local sugar farms are an Eastern Canadian tradition and allow visitors to make maple syrup taffy in the snow while working up an appetite for a large stack of pancakes dripping with the first batch of syrup. The three grades of maple syrup are light, medium, and dark. The light grade is produced early in the season and the darker grade at the end of the season, which is signaled by buds bursting on the trees. The darker the syrup the more concentrated the flavour. One of the best ways to enjoy maple syrup is drizzled over vanilla ice cream or added instead of sugar in a cup of coffee. If you wish to include maple sugar in baked goods, substitute ½ cup (125 ml) syrup for 1 cup (250 ml) of the sugar and reduce liquids by 3 Tbsp. (45 ml) for every cup substituted.

Strawberries – As the weather warms and the sun makes a more regular appearance, bright red, shiny-skinned strawberries begin to fill the market. With their sweet perfume wafting through the air, it is hard to resist buying several flats of these gorgeous berries. As with most foods at their prime, fresh local strawberries are best eaten simply, just by themselves, or with light syrup or a bit of cream. If you do buy a flat or two, make freezer jam or bake a pie. When buying your berries, look for bright, shiny fruit with fresh green stems and intense fragrance. Ideally you should use your strawberries right away, but if you have to store them in the refrigerator, keep them dry. First, pick through the berries, discarding any mouldy ones. Line a container or flat box with paper towels and place berries on top. Cover with more paper towel and seal with a lid or cover with plastic. Wash berries immediately before using them.

Spring

Spring greens with wild garlic, honey dressing

Grilled asparagus with bocconcini

Fresh pea soup

Cucumber mint soup

Fiddlehead quiche

Asparagus canneloni

Farfalle with goat cheese, baby spinach, and pine nuts

Fresh linguine with peas and mint

Delicate spring salmon

Pan-fried trout with sage butter

Butterflied lamb with mint pesto

Pine-nut-crusted rack of lamb

Spring chicken with morels

Roast chicken with lemon and thyme

Maple butter tarts

Maple custard

Ottawa Valley strawberry rhubarb pie

Strawberries with honeyed lemon syrup

Spring greens with a wild garlic, honey dressing

Serving size: 4

Dressing

½ cup	light olive oil	125 ml
3 Tbsp	fresh lemon juice	45 ml
1½ tsp	chopped wild minced garlic	10 ml
1 Tbsp	honey	15 ml
	salt and pepper to taste	

Salad

8	handfuls spring greens	8
½ cup	edible flowers	125 ml
⅓ cup	toasted pine nuts	100 ml
8 oz	goat cheese, crumbled	250 g

1 Place all dressing ingredients in a glass jar with a tight-fitting lid and shake well to combine.

2 Toss the salad greens with the desired amount of dressing. Divide among plates and sprinkle with edible flowers, pine nuts, and goat cheese.

Ottawa is known for its beautiful spring flowers, so why not include some edible varieties in your salad. Pansies and dianthus are pretty and tasty, too.

Grilled asparagus with bocconcini

1 Tbsp	fresh lemon juice	15 ml
¼ cup	finely diced red onion	50 ml
1 Tbsp	chopped fresh parsley	15 ml
¼ tsp	salt	1 ml
¼ tsp	freshly ground pepper	1 ml
4 Tbsp	olive oil	50 ml
1 pound	asparagus, bottoms trimmed	500 g
8	small bocconcini balls	8
2 Tbsp	chopped fresh chives	25 ml

1 In a medium bowl, whisk together the lemon juice, red onion, parsley, salt, and pepper. Gradually whisk in 3 tablespoons of olive oil. Reserve.

2 Bring a frying pan of water to a boil and blanch asparagus for 1 minute. Drain and place in ice-water bath for 1 to 2 minutes to retain colour. Drain and dry with paper towels. The recipe can be prepared to this point several hours before serving.

3 Toss asparagus with the remaining olive oil.

4 Heat a grill or the barbeque and grill asparagus until just tender and lightly browned.

5 Divide the grilled asparagus among 4 plates and arrange the bocconcini on top. Drizzle with vinaigrette and garnish with chives and chive flowers.

Bocconcini is fresh mozzarella that pairs beautifully with spring's choicest vegetable.

Fresh pea soup

3 cups	low-sodium chicken stock	750 ml
½	medium onion, finely diced	½
1	clove garlic	1
1⅓ cups	shelled fresh peas	325 ml
½ cup	plain yogurt	125 ml
	salt and pepper to taste	
¼ cup	finely diced radish as garnish	50 ml
	pea greens as garnish	

1 In a medium saucepan, bring the chicken stock to a boil and add the onion. Reduce the heat and simmer for about 10 minutes.

2 Add the fresh peas and simmer until the peas are bright green and tender but not mushy, about 8 to 10 minutes.

3 Using a blender, puree the peas and broth. Strain the soup through a wide mesh sieve into a medium-sized bowl, pressing the crushed peas through with the back of a spoon. Place bowl in an ice-water bath immediately and stir until cooled. This will set the bright green colour of the soup. Cover and chill in refrigerator.

4 Just before serving, add the yogurt and stir to blend. Season to taste with salt and pepper. Garnish with radish and fresh pea greens.

It always seems such a shame to mash up fresh green peas, but this soup is truly worth it! It is light, simple, and refreshing. You can purchase pea greens at specialty produce stands and Asian grocers.

Cucumber mint soup

Serving size: 4

1 Tbsp	butter	15 ml
1	large yellow onion, diced	1
2	cloves garlic, minced	2
8	cucumbers, peeled, seeded, and roughly chopped	8
4 cups	chicken stock	1 l
1 cup	plain yogurt	250 ml
1 cup	cream	250 ml
½ cup	mint, chopped	125 ml
1 Tbsp	lemon juice	15 ml
	salt and pepper to taste	

1 Sauté the onion in butter in a medium saucepan over medium-high heat until translucent. Add the garlic and stir to combine with the onion.
2 Add the cucumbers and the chicken. Bring to a boil, then reduce to a low simmer for 5 minutes. Remove from heat and let cool to room temperature.
3 Puree the soup. Stir in yogurt, cream, chopped mint, and lemon juice. Season with salt and pepper. Chill before serving.

Field cucumbers are best for this recipe as they are more flavourful and have fewer seeds than English cucumbers.

Fiddlehead quiche

5	sheets phyllo pastry	5
⅓ cup	butter, clarified	75 ml
1½ cups	half and half	375 ml
3	large eggs	3
1 cup	fiddleheads, blanched	250 ml
¾ cup	grated gruyere cheese	225 ml
⅛ tsp	nutmeg	1 ml
	salt and pepper to taste	

1 Preheat oven to 375°F.

2 Clarify butter by melting it in the microwave or on top of the stove. Skim the foam off the melted butter. Spoon or carefully pour the clear melted butter into another dish, discarding the milky solids at the bottom.

3 Brush the phyllo sheets, one at a time, with a small amount of clarified butter. Tear each sheet of phyllo in half lengthwise and lay them across a lightly oiled 9-inch pie plate. Criss-cross sheets of phyllo to evenly cover the base of the pie plate. Fold the overhanging edges of the phyllo inwards to form a crumpled-looking border.

4 Spread the grated cheese evenly over the base of the pastry. Arrange the fiddleheads on top. Beat together eggs, half and half, salt, pepper, and nut-meg. Pour over fiddleheads and bake for 45 to 50 minutes until puffed and golden. Let cool for 5 to 10 minutes before cutting. The quiche may be served warm or cold.

Using phyllo pastry instead of shortcrust pastry makes this quiche light and crisp. If phyllo begins to brown too quickly, lay strips of tin foil over the top of the pastry. If you can't find fiddleheads, asparagus is a good seasonal alternative.

Asparagus cannelloni

½ cup	butter	125 ml
6 Tbsp	flour	75 ml
	salt and pepper to taste	
4 cups	milk, heated	1 l
¼ tsp	fresh ground nutmeg	1 ml
2	bay leaves	2
1½ cups	grated Parmigiano-Reggiano	375 ml
10	sheets fresh lasagne noodles, parboiled and tossed with	10
1 tsp	olive oil	5 ml
8	slices prosciutto, coarsely chopped	8
2 pounds	asparagus, trimmed and blanched	900 g
4 Tbsp	freshly chopped parsley	60 ml

1 Preheat oven to 375°F.

2 For the white sauce, melt the butter in a large saucepan over medium-high heat. Whisk in flour and cook for 1 minute. Gradually add the warmed milk, whisking constantly. Add the bay leaves, salt, pepper, and nutmeg. Stir with a wooden spoon, scraping into the corners of the pot, until sauce thickly coats the back of a spoon. Once thickened, stir in 1 cup of the Parmigiano-Reggiano and the chopped prosciutto. Remove from the heat and set aside.

3 Spread 4 tablespoons of sauce in the bottom of a large (13 x 9-inch) oiled lasagne dish. Cut the lasagne noodles into 4-inch lengths and place a small bundle of blanched asparagus across the width of each noodle. Spoon 2 table-spoons of sauce over the asparagus and roll up the cannelloni. Place in the lasagne dish and continue, placing the cannelloni side by side.

4 Cover the prepared cannelloni with the rest of the sauce and sprinkle with the remaining ½ cup of cheese. Bake uncovered until golden and bubbly, approximately 30 to 40 minutes. Garnish with parsley.

Farfalle with goat cheese, baby spinach, and pine nuts

Serving size: 4

1 pound	farfalle pasta	450 g
4 Tbsp	olive oil	50 ml
2	cloves garlic, thinly sliced	2
⅛ tsp	chili peppers, crushed	1 ml
4 cups	baby spinach leaves, washed and dried	1 l
4 oz	goat cheese, crumbled	100 g
½ cup	pine nuts, toasted	

1 Cook pasta according to package directions until *al dente* and drain. Set aside.
2 Using the empty pasta pot, heat the olive oil, garlic, and chilis. Sauté briefly until garlic becomes fragrant, being careful not to let the garlic brown.
3 Add the spinach and reserved pasta to the pot. Toss to coat with the oil and allow the spinach to wilt and the pasta to warm through. Garnish with goat cheese and toasted pine nuts. Serve immediately.

A quick and easy pasta dish with great colour and flavour.

Fresh linguine with peas and mint

Serving size: 4

2 Tbsp	butter	25 ml
1	slice pancetta, cut into small pieces, optional	1
1	clove garlic, sliced in half	1
1 cup	shelled peas, blanched	250 ml
2 Tbsp	chopped fresh mint	25 ml
	salt and pepper to taste	
1 pound	fresh linguine, cooked and drained	500 g

1   In a large frying pan, melt the butter and crisp the bacon over moderate heat. Add the garlic and the peas and let cook for 1 minute. Remove the garlic and discard.

2   Add the mint, salt, pepper, and the drained, reserved pasta to the pan. Toss to coat. Serve immediately in warm bowls, garnished with fresh parmesan cheese.

This is best made with freshly shelled peas, blanched quickly to set their colour.

Delicate spring salmon

1 Tbsp	olive oil	15 ml
4	large shallots or 1 small onion, peeled and thinly sliced	4
2	medium carrots, in large dice	2 ml
2	yellow peppers, coarsely diced	2
1	bay leaf	1
¼ cup	chopped fresh dill	50 ml
½ cup	low-sodium chicken broth	125 ml
¼ cup	dry white wine, optional	50 ml
1 cup	diced asparagus	250 ml
4	pieces salmon fillet, skin removed	4
	salt and pepper to taste	
4 cups	cooked jasmine rice	1 l
¼ cup	chopped fresh parsley	50 ml
	flat-leaf parsley and lemon wedges for garnish	

1 In a large frying pan with a tight-fitting lid, heat the oil and add the shallots and carrots. Sauté for 5 minutes or until onion is soft and carrots are tender-crisp. Add the bay leaf, dill, broth, and wine. Bring to a boil.

2 Reduce the heat, add the diced asparagus and yellow peppers and lay the fish fillets over the vegetables. Season lightly with salt and pepper. Cover the pan and simmer slowly, adding a little more wine, or chicken stock, if necessary. The fish is done when the flesh is just slightly underdone, about 7 to 10 minutes.

3 Remove the cooked salmon to a warm plate and discard the bay leaf. Add the cooked rice to the frying pan and stir to warm through. Serve the salmon fillets on top of the rice mixture. Garnish with parsley and lemon.

This makes a perfect, light springtime meal.

Pan-fried trout with sage butter

Serving size: 4

3 Tbsp	butter	45 ml
1 Tbsp	olive oil	15 ml
1	large sprig fresh sage, leaves separated	1
¼ cup	flour	50 ml
	salt and pepper to taste	
4	fresh whole trout, cleaned	4 ml
2	lemons	2
¼ cup	chopped parsley	50 ml

1 In a large frying pan, heat the butter and olive oil over medium-high heat. Add the sage leaves and fry until crisp.

2 Meanwhile, season the flour with the salt and pepper. Lightly season the interior of the fish as well. Lightly coat the trout with the flour and add the fish to the frying pan. Cook until trout is golden on both sides and flesh flakes, approximately 5 to 8 minutes. Serve with fresh lemon and some chopped parsley.

This is wonderful simply served with couscous and a squeeze of fresh lemon.

Butterflied lamb with mint pesto

Serves 8

3	cloves of garlic	3
2 cups	mint leaves	500 ml
¼ cup	chopped chives	50 ml
½ cup + 1–2 tsp	olive oil	125 ml + 5–10 ml
1 (5–6 lb)	leg of lamb, trimmed, boned, and butterflied	1 (2.5–3 kg)
	salt and pepper to taste	

1   In food processor or using mortar and pestle, combine garlic, mint, chives, and ½ cup of oil until it forms a loose paste.

2   Season the lamb generously with salt and pepper. Cover the cut side of the meat with the pesto. Roll up the lamb and tie securely with kitchen string at intervals of 2–3 inches (5–7.5 cm). Cover and refrigerate for at least an hour. Bring to room temperature before roasting.

3   Preheat oven to 450°F. In a roasting pan, heat the oil and brown the lamb on all sides. Transfer the roasting pan to the oven and roast for 15 minutes. Reduce the oven temperature to 350°F and continue to roast, basting every 10 to 15 minutes, until a meat thermometer inserted in the thickest portion registers 125°–130°F for rare to medium rare, about 45 minutes. Transfer to a cutting board and let rest, loosely covered with aluminum foil, for 10 minutes before carving.

4   Remove the strings and carve the lamb across the grain into thin slices. Serve with the natural juices.

Butterflying meat creates an even thickness and allows for more even cooking. Rolling the lamb with the pesto infuses this roast from within.

Pine-nut-crusted rack of lamb

Serving size: 4

¼ cup	toasted pine nuts, chopped	50 ml
2 Tbsp	bread crumbs	25 ml
2 Tbsp	finely chopped fresh parsley	25 ml
2	frenched lamb racks	2
	salt and pepper to taste	
1 Tbsp	olive oil	15 ml
1 Tbsp	dijon mustard	15 ml
1 Tbsp	honey	15 ml

1 Preheat oven to 375°F.

2 Combine nuts, breadcrumbs, and parsley. Rub lamb racks with salt and pepper. Heat oil in a large frying pan over medium-high heat. Sear the racks on all sides until browned. Transfer to a small roasting pan and let cool for a few minutes so they are easier to handle.

3 Combine mustard and honey, spread onto the fat side of the lamb racks and press the nut mixture into the mustard mixture. Stand the racks, crusted side up, leaning against each other, and roast for 15 to 20 minutes or until crust is golden and the meat is cooked medium rare. Let rest 5 minutes before carving.

Lamb is classic springtime fare. The coating of breadcrumbs and pine nuts adds a welcome crunch.

Spring chicken with morels and fresh peas

Serving size: 4

4 Tbsp	olive oil	50 ml
10	green onions, chopped in 1-inch pieces	10
2	cloves garlic, minced	2
4	carrots, finely sliced	4
2 cups	fresh morels, whole	500 ml
1 cup	dry white wine	250 ml
1 cup	chicken stock	250 ml
4	free-range chicken breasts, bone in and skin on	4
	salt and pepper to taste	
1 cup	heavy cream	250 ml
1 Tbsp	lemon zest, finely grated	15 ml
1 cup	shelled peas	250 ml
2 Tbsp	chopped parsley	30 ml
1 lb	parpadelle pasta	450 g

1 Gently rinse morels in colander under running water. Drain and dry with paper towel.

2 Brush chicken breasts with 1 tablespoon of the oil; season well with salt and pepper. In another frying pan or on a cast-iron grill, brown the chicken pieces, skin side down first, for about 3 to 4 minutes. Turn the chicken and cook for another 5 to 10 minutes or until cooked through and juices run clear. Remove chicken and reserve in a warm oven.

3 Add the remaining olive oil to the frying pan, lower the heat, and gently sauté the onions, garlic, and carrots for about 3 minutes. Increase the heat and add the morels. Cook until softened, about another 3 minutes. Add the white wine and chicken stock. Boil until reduced by half.

4 Add the cream and grated lemon zest to the reduced stock, and boil until reduced by half. Then add the peas and cook for 2 to 3 minutes. Season to taste.

5 Cook pasta according to package directions. Drain and serve with chicken and morel sauce. Garnish generously with freshly chopped parsley.

Morels are a unique springtime ingredient. Indulge while you can!

Roast chicken with lemon and thyme

Serving size: 4

1 5–6 lb	roasting chicken	2–3 kg
	salt and pepper to taste	
1	large bunch fresh thyme	1
1	lemon, halved	1
1	head garlic, halved	1
2 Tbsp	butter	25 ml

1   Preheat oven to 425°F.
2   Remove giblets from chicken and rinse the bird inside and out. With paper towel, dry the chicken inside and out.
3   Generously season the chicken with salt and pepper inside and out. Stuff the cavity with the thyme, lemon, and garlic.
4   Place a tablespoon of butter under the skin of each breast, working your fingers under the skin, starting at the neck cavity.
5   Tie the legs together with kitchen string and tuck the wing tips under the body of the chicken.
6   Roast the chicken for 1½ hours or until the juices run clear.
7   Let the chicken rest, covered with foil, for 5 minutes before carving. Serve with the roasted garlic.

Nothing is more comforting than a simple roast chicken seasoned with fresh herbs.

Maple butter tarts

Pastry

¾ cup	vegetable shortening	175 ml
¼ cup	butter	50 ml
2 cups	flour	500 ml
¾ tsp	salt	3 ml
¼ cup	cold orange juice	50 ml

Filling

2 Tbsp	butter	25 ml
1 cup	brown sugar	250 ml
¼ cup + 2 Tbsp	maple syrup	50 ml
½ cup	currants	125 ml
2	eggs, beaten	2
½ tsp	vanilla	2.5 ml

1 Preheat oven to 400°F.

2 Prepare pastry by combining the flour and salt in a food processor bowl or large mixing bowl. Add the chilled butter and shortening and cut into the flour using the sharp blade of the food processor or 2 knives until the chunks of butter are the size of large peas. Add the orange juice 1 tablespoon at a time. The moment the dough starts to come together, stop working it and wrap it in plastic. Flatten the dough into a disk and chill it for at least an hour.

3 Roll out pastry on a lightly floured surface. Cut circles, using a 3–4-inch round pastry cutter, and place in tart shells or directly into a standard muffin tin. Reserve, covered, in the refrigerator.

4 In a medium bowl, beat butter, brown sugar, maple syrup, and vanilla. Set aside.

5 Place currants in a small pot and cover with 1 inch of water. Bring to a boil and drain. Immediately add the currants to the sugar mixture and stir to melt the butter.

6 Whisk in beaten eggs and divide mixture among tart shells, filling each ¾ of the way full. Bake for 12 to 15 minutes or until pastry is golden brown and the tops of tarts are set but still jiggle in the centre slightly. Allow to cool completely before removing from pan.

These sweet, runny tarts are truly a Canadian confection, and thought to be a variation on Quebec's sugar pie.

Maple custard

Serving size: 6

1 cup	sugar	250 ml
½ cup	water	125 ml
3	eggs	3
2	egg yolks	2
½ Tbsp	Grand Marnier	7 ml
½ cup	maple syrup	125 ml
3 cups	heavy cream	750 ml

1 Combine sugar and water in a small saucepan over medium heat. Without stirring, let the sugar melt and caramelize until it starts to turn a medium-brown colour. Swirl the pot to mix the browning sugar and remove from the heat. Carefully add 2 tablespoons of water to the saucepan, continuing to swirl. The caramel will bubble and spit when the cold water hits it. Divide the caramel among 6 dessert ramekins or 6-ounce custard cups. Set aside but do not refrigerate.

2   Preheat the oven to 300°F. Whisk eggs, yolks, Grand Marnier, and syrup together in a small bowl. Warm the cream then whisk some of the cream into the egg mixture to temper the eggs. Return the egg and cream mixture to the rest of the cream, pouring in a slow steady stream. Whisk to combine.

3   Pour custard into the ramekins. Place the filled ramekins into a shallow roasting pan on the middle rack of the preheated oven. Pour water around the ramekins in the roasting pan to a depth of about 1 inch. Bake for 40 minutes or until the custard is nearly set in the middle. Custards should still jiggle in the centre when lightly shaken. Remove from the water bath and let custards cool on the counter for about 1 hour. Cover with plastic wrap and chill for at least 4 hours before unmolding.

4   To serve, run a sharp knife around each custard cup. Place a plate upside down on top of the ramekin and invert quickly. The caramel from the bottom of the ramekin should flow over the custard.

This recipe is easy, not too "eggy," and shows off the flavour of maple syrup.

Ottawa Valley strawberry rhubarb pie

Serving size: 6

Pastry

1 cup	shortening	250 ml
2 cups	flour	500 ml
¾ tsp	salt	3 ml
¼ cup	cold orange juice	50 ml

Filling

2 Tbsp	cornstarch	25 ml
1 cup	sugar	250 ml
1	egg, beaten	1
3 cups	strawberries, halved	750 ml
1 cup	rhubarb, cut into 1-inch pieces	250 ml
1 Tbsp	butter	15 ml

1 Prepare pastry by combining the flour and salt in a large bowl. Add the chilled butter and shortening and cut into the flour using the sharp blade of the food processor or 2 knives until the chunks of butter are the size of large peas. Add the orange juice 1 tablespoon at a time. The moment the dough starts to come together, stop working it and wrap it in plastic. Flatten the dough into a disk and chill it for at least an hour.

2 Roll out ½ of the pastry for the bottom crust. Use it to line a 9-inch pie plate. Roll out remainder for a top crust.

3 Combine cornstarch, sugar, and beaten egg and mix with the fruit.

4 Place fruit in pie plate and pour the rest of the egg mixture over top of the fruit. Dot with butter and cover with pastry. With a sharp knife, cut air vent in the pastry top.

5 Bake at 400°F for about 45 minutes or until golden and bubbly. Let cool before slicing.

> **The tartness of the rhubarb balances the sweetness of the berries for a wonderful springtime treat.**

Strawberries with honeyed lemon syrup

Serving size: 4

¼ cup	honey	50 ml
½	small lemon, juiced	½
1 quart	strawberries, hulled and sliced	1 l
	lemon zest for garnish	

1 In a small saucepan over moderate heat, melt the honey and add the lemon juice. Let simmer gently for about 2 minutes. Take off the heat to let cool and allow the flavours to blend.

2 To serve, drizzle over strawberries and garnish with lemon zest.

> **Nothing can compare to a local strawberry in season. Rather than cook out that fresh flavour, enjoy them in the raw drizzled with a simple syrup.**

Summer

at Granville Island Market

DIRECT FROM THE ORCH

SWEET & JUIC

OKANAGA

Granville Island Public Market is a unique urban oasis located on the edge of downtown Vancouver and was intentionally created, in the early seventies, as a public space. The site of Granville Island was originally a large sandbar at the entrance to what is now known as False Creek. The value of the sandbar as industrial land became apparent to local businesspeople, and in 1915, the federal government approved the dredging and construction of "Industrial Island". In the years following, this "Industrial Island" became known as Granville Island and was the home of sawmills, ironworkers' forges, slaughterhouses, and other industrial and manufacturing activities.

By the early seventies, a new plan for the Island was envisioned; it would be transformed into a public space, incorporating a market, restaurants, theatres, studios, marinas, an art college, and a network of paths and parks. To link the Island's past with its bright new future, the industrial feel of the Island's heritage was maintained by utilizing architectural elements such as tin siding, cranes, exposed wooden beams, rail tracks, and steel pipes.

Today, when you arrive on the Island, you pass under the cool shadow of the Granville Street Bridge and walk the boardwalk past moored boats of all sizes. The Net Loft, one of several colourful buildings on the island, is home to shops, many featuring unique items.

Just a few steps away from the shops is the market itself. As you enter, the fresh aroma of roasted coffee beans hits, and your eyes are immediately drawn to the exotic mix of flowers standing in metal buckets and hanging in bunches from the rafters. Farmers from the Fraser Valley have tables full of juicy, fat blackberries and just-picked corn on the cob. There is even a vendor who sells at least 10 kinds of organic salad greens that you can mix yourself. The seafood shops, featuring whole fresh salmon, are always a popular attraction. You can even buy a live Dungeness crab and have it cooked for you while you shop; buy some lemons and some prepared dips and have a feast out on the dock overlooking False Creek!

Summer

What to Look for at Granville Island

The summer months in Vancouver are celebrated and cherished for as long as possible. The sun is warm and the ocean breeze refreshing. Granville Island Public Market is alive with street performers, locals, and tourists. Produce stands are stacked with juicy peaches from the Okanagan, fat blackberries, and sweet corn. Wild salmon is especially good during the summer months, so if you can't catch your own, head down to the market and indulge.

Tomatoes – Once you've tasted a simple summer tomato salad, how could a mealy supermarket tomato ever compare? Tomatoes are the perfect example for eating within the seasons. Tomatoes peak at the end of summer, after long, hot days soaking up as much sun as possible. Public markets are the place to find a number of varieties of tomatoes not available at the supermarket, each with its own distinct flavour and use. Look for tomatoes that smell good, feel firm, and are heavy for their size. Odd shapes and growth cracks do not affect the flavour of a tomato; they simply add character. Never store tomatoes in the refrigerator or they quickly become mealy and tasteless.

Corn – It wouldn't be summer without farm fresh corn on the cob. Whether boiled, steamed, or barbecued, corn on the cob is best rolled in butter and sprinkled with salt. Sure, you can use herbed or spiced butters, but be careful not to overwhelm the sweet corn taste. If you've had your fill of cob corn make a summer corn chowder. When purchasing corn, look for ears that have pale stem ends and fresh-looking silk at the tip. Kernels should be moist and plump. Refrigerate corn in its husk and use as soon as possible.

Green Beans – During the warm months of summer, green beans are at their best. Brilliant green, and tender when cooked, string beans are wonderful dressed as a salad or a crunchy side dish. Look for beans that are crisp and firm. Boil in salted water until just tender. If you must store your fresh beans, place them in a paper bag inside a plastic bag. The paper bag absorbs any excess moisture, and the plastic keeps the beans from going limp.

Summer Squash – Summer squash come in many shapes and sizes, the most common being the green zucchini. Keep an eye out for other varieties at the public market, such as yellow zucchini and green and yellow pattypan squash. The flavour of all summer squash is similar, but the difference in colour and shape can add great variety to your plate. Try long slices of zucchini basted with olive oil and roasted or grilled, or individual pattypans whole on kebabs or cut into chunks. Summer squash has a soft, smooth skin and a delicate flavour. Look for summer squash that are firm with shiny, smooth, unblemished skins. Zucchini past its prime will taste bitter when cooked. Refridgerate in a plastic bag.

Sweet Bell Peppers – Green, red, yellow, or orange, bell peppers are sweet and plump in the summer. Green peppers are, in fact, immature red, yellow, or orange peppers and therefore less sweet than the other colours. Use them to add colour and crunch to recipes. Red and yellow peppers add sweetness when simply tossed into a pasta dish or grilled on the barbeque. Look for thick-walled, firm peppers with bright green stems. Peppers last a surprisingly long time when kept in a plastic bag in the crisper of the refrigerator.

Yukon Gold Potatoes – Yukon Gold potatoes are yellow-fleshed medium-starch potatoes that have a buttery taste without the butter. You can bake, steam, sauté, or boil Yukons, and their skin is tender enough to leave on even when mashed. Fresh potatoes have moist, tender skins with few scuffs and are very firm. Generally, smaller potatoes have better flavour and texture than older, larger potatoes. Avoid sprouting potatoes or those that are tinged with green. (The green colour occurs when potatoes are exposed to light for a prolonged period. The green flesh can be toxic in large quantities.) Keep potatoes in a cool, dark environment. Do not store them in the fridge, where the starch in the potato will turn to sugar, resulting in an unpleasantly sweet flavour.

Wild Pacific Salmon – Pacific salmon are a unique species. Unlike Atlantic salmon, which spawn several times in their lifetime, a Pacific salmon will return to the place of its birth only once and then die. Different varieties of Pacific salmon each "run" at different times of the year, returning to specific rivers to spawn. Given this incredible life cycle, West Coast market-goers are likely to find fresh salmon available most of the year. The summer months, however, seem to be the most bountiful.

Chinook: Also known as spring salmon, Chinook is the largest species of salmon and, due to its high fat content, is very flavourful. The colour of its flesh ranges from ivory to deep red.

Coho: Full flavoured with a fine texture, Coho is most abundant during July and August.

Sockeye: Popular sockeyes are known especially for their deep red flesh, which has a robust flavour and a small flake.

Chum and Pink: Chum and Pink salmon are smaller varieties with a milder, more delicate flavour. Their flesh is considerably lighter in colour than the larger species. Chum and Pink salmon are often served poached or steamed.

Fresh salmon have bright, clear eyes, moist skin with shiny scales, pink gills, flesh that springs back when pressed, and a fresh scent, reminiscent of the ocean.

Spot Prawns – If you have access to live spot prawns, indulge! Not only are they beautiful but also very sweet. They are best straight off the boat but you can also find them live at the market in tanks. Look for lively, active prawns – is an indication of how long they have been captive. The longer the prawns are in the tanks, the more likely their flesh will be mushy and not as sweet when cooked.

Dungeness crab – The season for this West Coast specialty begins in the spring after the crabs have molted but it takes a crab months before it fills its shell, providing eager consumers with its sweet, delicious meat. By the time summer rolls around at Granville Island, you can buy your crab live and then have it cooked on the spot, just in time for lunch! Look for active live crabs; crabs that have lingered too long in a tank will often be a bit sleepy and stressed. Cooked crab in its shell spoils quickly, so eat it right away. Buying cooked, shelled crab may be pricey, but you save time and buy only how much you need.

Melons – Melons aren't only for breakfast; think of them as an ingredient that can be paired with savoury foods as well as sweet. Imagine a light and refreshing melon salsa with warm, grilled scallops or roasted sea bass. Summer provides the best cantaloupes, honeydews, and watermelon. Casabas are another variety to try, with a delicate, sweet flavour and whitish flesh. When choosing netted melons, like cantaloupe, the background colour should be tan or golden, not green. Honeydew skin should be creamy yellow with a velvety feel. Generally, you will know a melon is ready to eat by its sweet fragrance. Watermelons, however, are tricky; when ripe, their colour is dull and their skin is hard. If you slap a ripe watermelon, it will sound like you're hitting a jug of water.

Peaches and Nectarines – A great peach or nectarine is one that drips with juice when you eat it. It should be deep golden yellow with or without a red blush and firm but not hard. Most peaches and nectarines you see in grocery stores have been picked early for the sake of shipping and durability. This practice, however, sacrifices flavour. Local producers selling at a public market can let the fruit ripen properly and develop sweetness. Look for firm fruit that gives slightly when gently pressed. Smell is important; both peaches and nectarines should have a wonderful perfume.

Blueberries – Blueberries are a wonderful summer treat. If you are lucky enough to find wild blueberries, indulge! Wild blueberries are about the size of a small pea yet burst with tremendous flavour. They are especially wonderful polka-dotted through pancakes. Look for berries that still have a powdery sheen to them. This powder is natural yeast and its presence indicates that the berries haven't been overly handled. Blueberries are fairly sturdy but must be kept cool and dry when stored. Store in a thin layer in the refrigerator covered with paper towel and plastic.

Blackberries and Raspberries – Blackberries run wild on the West Coast. Consequently, there is an abundant supply at Granville Island late in the summer. Cultivated raspberries make their appearance usually by late July. Both berries are excellent for jam, pie, over cereal, or simply eaten out of hand. Fully ripe berries have large plump drupelets – the little sacs that make up the berry – and a glorious scent. Ideally, ripe berries should be used right away, as they are fragile and don't store well. Keep berries refrigerated; laid out in a thin layer and covered with paper towel and plastic.

Summer

Wild blueberry pancakes

Raspberry blueberry jam

Warm green bean salad

Tomato crab salad

Dill mustard potato salad

Summer corn chowder

Goat cheese and roasted bell pepper tart

Spaghetti with cherry tomatoes and arugula

Roasted tomato sauce

Grilled polenta with braised bell peppers and spicy sausage

Grilled vegetable stacks with gorgonzola polenta

Smoked salmon hand rolls

Cedar-baked salmon

Salmon barbeque

Seared scallops with couscous and melon salsa

Spot prawn fettucine

Dungeness crab cakes

Rosemary scalloped potatoes

Yukon Gold mashed potatoes

Tomato mango avocado salsa

Blueberry cheesecake

Blackberry shortcake

Peach apricot galette

Wild blueberry pancakes

Serving Size: 4

2 cups	flour	500 ml
4 Tsp	baking powder	20 ml
4 Tbsp	brown sugar	50 ml
¼ cup	corn meal	50 ml
½ tsp	salt	2.5 ml
2 cups	milk	500 ml
1	egg, lightly beaten	1
4 Tbsp	butter, melted	50 ml
	plus extra for the grill	
2 cups	blueberries	500 ml

1   Mix together dry ingredients.
2   Add the wet ingredients to the flour mixture all at once and mix until just combined. Batter should be slightly lumpy. If necessary, add an extra tablespoon of milk at a time until batter is pourable. Let rest while the frying pan heats.
3   Add a bit of butter to the heated pan and spread over cooking surface. Ladle batter onto frying pan to form pancakes about 3 inches in diameter. Sprinkle the tops of pancakes with blueberries. Cook until bubbles appear on surface and undersides are golden brown. Flip pancakes and cook until undersides are golden brown.
4   Keep pancakes warm in the oven and continue with the rest of the batter. Makes about 20 pancakes.

If you can, make these pancakes with tiny, wild blueberries!

Raspberry blueberry jam

Serving Size: 4 cups

4 cups	raspberries, crushed	1 l
1 cup	blueberries, crushed	250 ml
5 cups	sugar	1.25 l
1	box Certo powdered pectin	57 g

1 In a large pot, combine crushed fruit with pectin and bring to a boil.
2 Add the sugar and stir. Bring back to a vigorous boil that doesn't reduce in intensity when stirred.
3 Ladle hot jam carefully into sterilized jars and seal.

This is really the only way to make jam. It is slightly runny and full of bright fresh fruit flavour. It doesn't have all the sugar that most recipes require so don't plan on keeping it for more than a year. That shouldn't be hard; you'll go through it pretty quickly because it's so good. It's also wonderful as a sauce with cheesecake.

Warm green bean salad

Serving Size: 4

1	small red onion, finely diced	1
1 Tbsp	olive oil	15 ml
2 Tbsp	balsamic vinegar	25 ml
	salt and pepper to taste	
1 pound	green beans, trimmed	454 g

1   In a serving bowl, lightly mix together the red onion, oil, vinegar, salt, and pepper.
2   Blanch the green beans in boiling water for about 2 minutes. They should be bright green and still slightly crunchy.
3   Drain the beans and add them directly to the serving bowl. Toss to coat with the dressing and serve immediately.

Use the freshest young green beans you can find for this recipe!

Tomato crab salad

½ pound	crab meat, picked over	250 g
1	red pepper, diced	1
½ cup	corn kernels, cooked	125 ml
⅛ Tsp	cayenne pepper	1 ml
1 Tbsp	chopped cilantro	15 ml
½ Tbsp	mayonnaise	7 ml
½ Tsp	lime juice	2.5 ml
2 large	tomatoes, thickly sliced	2
6	large basil leaves	6
	chives for garnish	

1 In a small bowl, gently mix together crab meat, red pepper, corn, cayenne pepper, cilantro, mayonnaise, and lime juice; set aside. Arrange tomatoes on a large platter or individual salad plates; top each tomato slice with a basil leaf and a mound of crab salad mixture. Garnish with fresh snipped chives.

Serve as a first course or with grilled meats and vegetables.

Dill mustard potato salad

Serving Size: 6

8	large Yukon Gold potatoes	8

Dressing

1 cup	dill pickles, diced	250 ml
1	small red onion, diced	1
½ cup	creamy dill mustard	125 ml
½ cup	plain yogurt	125 ml
2 Tbsp	mayonnaise	25 ml
	salt and pepper to taste	

1 Boil potatoes, whole, until just cooked though, about 20 to 30 minutes. Drain and cool under cold running water.

2 Meanwhile, mix together the rest of the ingredients and set aside.

3 Once the potatoes are completely cool, cut into chunks, leaving the skins on. Toss with the dressing and chill until serving.

If you cannot find prepared dill mustard, use dijon mustard and add chopped fresh dill to taste.

Summer corn chowder

2 Tbsp	butter	25 ml
1	large onion, diced	1
10	small new red potatoes, cut in half	10
1	bay leaf	1
2	sprigs fresh rosemary	2
2	sprigs fresh thyme	2
3	cobs corn	3
2 Tbsp	flour	25 ml
3 cups	milk	750 ml
1½ cups	half and half	375 ml
¼ tsp	cayenne pepper	1 ml
1	piece Parmigiano-Reggiano rind	1
1	small red pepper, diced	1
	salt and pepper to taste	
½ cup	freshly chopped parsley	125 ml

1 In a heavy pot, melt butter and sauté onion until translucent, about 5 min.
2 Add potatoes and herbs and stir to coat with onion mixture.
3 Cut the kernels off the cobs and add the kernels to the potato mixture. Cook for 2 minutes. With the blade of a knife, scrape the cobs over the soup pot to release the sweet corn milk.
4 Add the milk, half and half, and cayenne pepper. Bring the soup to a boil, then reduce to a simmer. Add the Parmigiano-Reggiano rind and simmer the soup until potatoes are tender, about 20 minutes.
5 Season with salt and pepper and stir in chopped parsley.

This soup is light and full of sweet corn flavour. The addition of the parmesan rind is a great flavour enhancer but it is not essential.

Goat cheese and roasted bell pepper tart

Serving Size: 6

Pastry

1¼ cups	all purpose flour	300 ml
⅛ tsp	salt	1 ml
¼ cup	butter	50 ml
1 tablespoon	shortening	15 ml
4½ tablespoons	ice water	70 ml

Filling

6	large bell peppers, red and yellow	6
2 Tbsp	olive oil	30 ml
8 oz	goat cheese	250 ml
½ cup	tapenade**	125 ml

1 Prepare pastry by combining the flour and salt in a food processor bowl or large mixing bowl. Add the chilled butter and shortening and cut into the flour using the sharp blade of the food processor or 2 knives until the chunks of butter are the size of large peas. Add the water 1 tablespoon at a time. The moment the dough starts to come together, stop working it and wrap it in plastic. Flatten the dough into a disk and chill it for at least an hour.

2 Preheat oven to 450°F.

3 Cut peppers in half and discard the seeds and tops.

4 Toss the peppers with oil and season with salt and pepper. Place peppers cut-side down on a parchment-lined baking sheet and roast until the skins have blackened, 15 to 20 minutes.

5 Immediately place the hot peppers in a bowl and cover with plastic wrap. Reduce oven temperature to 400°F.

6 While the peppers are steaming, roll out the pastry to a 10-inch circle. Trim ragged edges with a sharp knife. Set the rolled pastry on a parchment-lined baking sheet, cover, and chill until you're ready to assemble the tart.

7 Peel the peppers by slipping off and discarding the roasted skins. Thinly slice the skinned peppers and reserve.

8 Spread the goat cheese onto the rolled pastry, leaving an inch-wide border. Next spread the tapenade over the goat cheese. Lastly, cover the tapenade with the sliced peppers.

9 Placing one finger under the edge of the pastry, fold it upwards, and press down at the crease. Repeat this action every inch around the tart. The result will be a beautiful ruffled edge that will hold in the oven.

10 Bake for about 30 minutes or until the crust is golden brown.

** Tapenade is a chopped mixture of black and green olives, capers, garlic, anchovies, parsley, and olive oil. You can make it yourself or buy it pre-made at gourmet shops.

Try mixing grilled vegetables with the roasted peppers for added colour. To save time, use store-bought pastry.

Spaghetti with cherry tomatoes and arugula

Serving Size: 4

1 pound	spaghetti, cooked and drained	500 g
2 Tbsp	extra virgin olive oil	25 ml
1	clove garlic, minced	1
¼ tsp	crushed chili peppers	1 ml
	salt and pepper to taste	
40	cherry tomatoes	40
2 cups	raw arugula leaves, cleaned	500 ml
¼ cup	chopped fresh parsley	50 ml

1   Cook pasta according to package directions and reserve.

2   Meanwhile, in a large frying pan, heat the olive oil with the garlic and chili peppers. Add the tomatoes and toss to coat with the oil. Let cook for 5 to 10 minutes until warmed and the tomatoes begin to crack. Season with salt and pepper.

3   Add the arugula and toss to coat with the oil. Let the arugula wilt and add the reserved pasta. Toss to coat with oil and heat through.

4   Serve in warmed bowls and garnish with chopped parsley and freshly grated parmesan cheese.

This is a simple, colourful summer pasta that highlights the season's sweetest tomatoes. Use yellow, red, and orange cherry or pear-shaped tomatoes for the best presentation.

Roasted tomato sauce

Serving Size: 4

20	medium plum tomatoes	20
6	cloves garlic, peeled	6
3 Tbsp	olive oil	45 ml
	salt and pepper to taste	
2 Tbsp	chopped fresh thyme	25 ml
2 Tbsp	chopped fresh marjoram	25 ml

1   Preheat oven to 400°F. Cut tomatoes in half horizontally. Scoop out the halves and discard seeds. In a large bowl combine the tomatoes, garlic, olive oil, salt, and pepper. Thoroughly coat the tomatoes with the oil and arrange tomato halves cut-side up on a baking sheet, preferably lined with parchment paper (tomatoes tend to taste metallic if cooked directly on metal) or in a glass pan. Roast 30 to 40 minutes.

2   Remove tomatoes from the oven, turn them over, and pull off the skins with a pair of tongs. Return skinless tomato halves to the oven and roast for another 10 to 15 minutes.

3   Remove tomatoes from the oven and transfer to a heatproof bowl. Add any juices left on the pan and the chopped fresh herbs.

4   For a chunky sauce, simply mash the tomatoes with a fork. Serve hot over pasta or use as the base for pizza.

Roasting tomatoes intensifies their flavour and natural sweetness. Use this sauce as the base for a delicious tomato soup. Purée the sauce and add chicken stock until you have a desired consistency. Finish with some cream for added richness.

Grilled polenta with braised bell peppers and spicy sausage

Serving Size: 4

Polenta

7 cups	water	1.75 l
1 Tbsp	salt	15 ml
1⅔ cups	coarse ground cornmeal	400 ml

Sauce

1 Tbsp	olive oil	15 ml
3	spicy Italian sausages, cut into 1-inch pieces	3
4	large red peppers, in strips	4
4	large yellow peppers, in strips	4
1	large onion, sliced	1
	salt and pepper to taste	
2	cloves garlic, minced	2
1 can (28 oz)	diced tomatoes with juice	796 ml
1 Tbsp	tomato paste	15 ml
¼ cup	chopped fresh cilantro	50 ml

1 For the polenta, bring the water to a boil in a large heavy pot. Add the salt and pour in the cornmeal in a slow, steady stream while stirring with a whisk. Keep the water boiling and continue to stir with a wooden spoon for about 30 minutes or until the cornmeal forms a mass and pulls away from the sides of the pot. Be careful, the thickened polenta will boil and spit towards the end. Pour onto a large board or jelly roll pan and spread to 1½-inch thickness. Let cool and firm up.

2 In a large frying pan, heat the oil over medium-high heat. Brown the sausage and then reserve on a plate. Add the peppers, onion, salt, pepper, and garlic to the pan. Sauté 10 minutes, until the onions have softened and coloured slightly.

3   Stir in the crushed tomatoes and tomato paste. Return sausage to the pan and bring mixture to a boil. Reduce heat and simmer for 30 minutes or until peppers are soft and sauce has thickened. Stir in basil and season again.

4   Cut cooled polenta into squares and grill or sauté.

5   To serve, spoon pepper and sausage mixture over grilled polenta pieces.

You can make your own polenta or buy pre-made polenta sold in tubes. The packaged variety slices very well and comes in a variety of flavours.

Grilled vegetable stacks with gorgonzola polenta

Serving Size: 4

1	eggplant, sliced in ¼-inch rounds	1
½ tsp	salt	2.5 ml
2	medium red bell peppers, quartered with seeds removed	2
2	large zucchini, sliced lengthwise	2
12	fresh shiitake mushrooms, stems removed	12
¾ cup	extra virgin olive oil	175 ml
	salt and pepper to taste	

Polenta

7 cups	water	1.75 l
1 Tbsp	salt	15 ml
1⅔ cups	coarse-grained cornmeal	400 ml
½ cup	gorgonzola	125 ml

1   Preheat barbeque to high.
2   Season the eggplant slices with salt and let them rest in a colander for about 30 minutes. This will remove their characteristic bitterness. Wash the slices under running water and pat dry. Reserve.
3   In a large bowl, toss the eggplant slices, pepper, zucchini, and mushrooms with ½ cup of the olive oil. Grill until well marked and tender.
4   Arrange vegetable stacks by alternating slices and reserve in a warm oven.
5   Bring the water for the polenta to boil in a large, heavy pot. Add the salt and reduce the heat to medium high. Pour the cornmeal into the pot in a slow steady stream and stir with a whisk continuously.

6   Continue stirring with a wooden spoon until the mixture thickens and begins to pull cleanly away from the sides of the pot, about 20 to 30 minutes.

7   Stir in the gorgonzola and serve immediately with the reserved vegetable stacks.

This is a colourful vegetarian recipe that works well for entertaining.

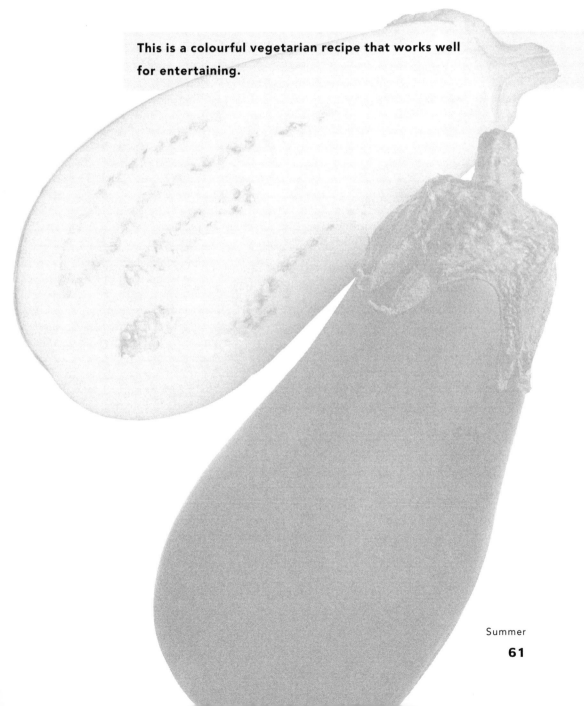

Smoked salmon hand rolls

Serving Size: 4

8	7 x 4-inch nori sheets	8
1 cup	sushi rice, polished short grain	250 ml
8	scallion greens	8
½ cup	daikon sprouts (optional)	125 ml
24	4-inch long peeled cucumber slices, cut matchstick size	24
16	slices smoked salmon	16
2 Tbsp	prepared wasabi paste	25 ml
½ cup	soy sauce	125 ml
¼ cup	pickled ginger	50 ml

1 Cook sushi rice according to package directions and reserve.

2 Pass a sheet of nori over a hot stove element a couple of times. This will lightly toast the nori. Spread each sheet of nori with the sushi rice so that you have a 1-inch strip across the middle of the sheet.

3 Divide the vegetables and salmon among the 8 sheets and roll to form a cone shape.

4 Serve with wasabi, soy sauce, and pickled ginger.

A popular West Coast adaptation of an imported favourite.

Cedar-baked salmon

Serving Size: 4

4	portions (6–8 oz) salmon fillet, or a whole side (2 lb/1 kg)	4 (180–250 g)
¼ cup	olive oil	50 ml
1	lemon, juiced with zest removed	1
	salt and pepper to taste	

1   Marinate the salmon pieces in the olive oil, lemon, salt, and pepper for
1 hour at room temperature. Meanwhile, soak an untreated cedar plank,
a little wider and longer than the fish, for about 2 hours. Place a weight on
the plank so it is completely submerged.

2   Heat the oven to 450°F and heat the plank for about 5 to 10 minutes.
Remove the salmon from the marinade and bake on the plank until
cooked through; roughly 10 minutes per inch thickness of fish.

**This is a classic BC salmon recipe that is an adaptation
of the First Nations' traditional method of roasting
salmon on cedar stakes over an open fire.**

Salmon barbeque

½ cup	butter, melted	125 ml
4 Tbsp	lemon juice	60 ml
1 Tbsp	fresh oregano or ¼ tsp (1 ml) dried	15 ml
1	side salmon, filleted, skin on	1
	salt and pepper to taste	

1 Melt the butter in a small saucepan and add the lemon juice and oregano. Brush this basting sauce over the salmon flesh.

2 Season the salmon generously with salt and pepper and let the salmon stand at room temperature for about 1 hour.

3 Preheat barbeque to medium.

4 Place the salmon, skin side down, on a piece of heavy aluminium foil. Crimp up the edges of the foil to form a tray. Place this foil tray with the salmon on the preheated barbeque and cover. Baste the fish every 5 minutes and check for doneness regularly. Salmon is cooked when it flakes with a fork and is medium rare in the centre, about 25 to 30 minutes. Salmon will continue to cook while off the grill.

5 To serve, cut pieces from the fillet and lift the meat from the skin.

If you use individual fillets for the recipe, reduce the cooking time accordingly.

Seared scallops with couscous and melon salsa

Serving Size: 4

20	sea scallops	20
1 cup	chicken stock	250 ml
1 cup	couscous	250 ml
1 Tbsp	chopped fresh parsley	15 ml
2 Tbsp	olive oil	25 ml

Salsa

1 cup	cantaloupe in ½-inch dice	250 ml
1 cup	honeydew melon in ½-inch dice	250 ml
¼ cup	finely diced red onion	50 ml
¼ cup	freshly chopped cilantro	50 ml
	salt and pepper to taste	
1	lemon, juiced	1
1	lime for garnish	1

1 Season the scallops with salt and reserve.
2 For the salsa, combine the melons, onion, chopped cilantro, and lemon juice. Season lightly with salt and pepper. Set aside.
3 In a small pot, bring the stock to a boil. Remove from heat and pour in the couscous. Cover and let rest for about 10 to 15 minutes. Fluff with a fork and stir in the chopped parsley.
4 Heat the oil in a large frying pan, on high. Place the scallops in the pan, leaving lots of space between them. Sear for 1 minute, until edges are crisp and deep golden. Turn and sear the other side. Remove from heat and keep scallops warm.
5 Arrange couscous on plates. Top with salsa, seared scallops, and lime.

This is a refreshing light meal, perfect for a warm summer evening.

Spot prawn fettucine

Serving size: 4

20	large spot prawns, peeled and deveined	20
1 Tbsp	butter	15 ml
4 Tbsp	olive oil	60 ml
	salt and pepper to taste	
½ cup	white wine	125 ml
1	large garlic clove, minced	1
4	large Roma tomatoes, diced	2
4 Tbsp	parsley, chopped	50 ml
1 pound	dried fettucine	500 g
2 Tbsp	chopped parsley for garnish	25 ml
4	lemon wedges for garnish	4

1 Boil water for pasta. Peel and devein shrimp and set aside.
2 While pasta is cooking, melt butter with olive oil in a large frying pan. Add shrimp and sauté for 2 to 3 minutes until they just turn pink. Remove shrimp from the pan and reserve.
3 Pour the wine into the pan, scraping up any brown bits from the bottom and let reduce by about half. Add garlic, tomato, and parsley and stir until fragrant, about 1 minute. Add the shrimp back to the sauce to warm through.
4 Drain pasta once it is done and put it into a warmed serving bowl. Immediately add reserved shrimp and sauce and toss well. Garnish with additional chopped parsley and lemon.

Fresh, sweet spot prawns make this dish exceptional.

Dungeness crab cakes

Serving Size: 4

½ pound	Dungeness crab meat	250g
½ cup	red onion, diced	125 ml
2 Tbsp	chopped fresh parsley	25 ml
¼ cup	red bell pepper, diced	50 ml
½ Tbsp	chopped fresh cilantro	7 ml
¼ tsp	dijon mustard	1 ml
1 ½ Tbsp	mayonnaise	20 ml
	salt and pepper to taste	
2	dashes tabasco sauce	2
1 ½ Tbsp	fine dry breadcrumbs for coating	20 ml
1	egg	1
1 cup	fine dry breadcrumbs	250 ml
	canola oil for frying	

Cayenne Mayonnaise

1 cup	mayonnaise	250 ml
½ Tbsp	cayenne pepper	7.5 ml
	squeeze of lemon to taste	

1 Combine all the ingredients except for the breadcrumbs reserved for coating. The mixture will seem very wet due to the egg.

2 On a tray or large plate, spread out the breadcrumbs. Using one hand, scoop up ¼ cup of the crab cake mixture and drop it onto the bread-crumbs. Using your clean hand, sprinkle breadcrumbs over the crab cake mound. Pick up the coated mound and very gently shape into a 2-inch diameter cake, adding more crumbs if necessary to coat evenly. Makes about 12 crab cakes.
   Pan fry the crab cakes in a heavy frying pan (cast iron works very well for this) using just a little oil. Brown nicely on both sides. Serve warm.

3 Meanwhile, in a small bowl, mix together mayonnaise, cayenne pepper, and lemon juice. Serve with crab cakes.

Summer

Rosemary scalloped potatoes

4	large Yukon Gold potatoes, thinly sliced	4
1 Tbsp	oil	15 ml
½	small onion	½
3	sprigs fresh rosemary	3
	salt and pepper to taste	
	half and half, enough to cover	

1 Preheat the oven to 375°F.

2 Lightly butter a small baking dish or 8-inch pie plate. In a small frying pan, heat oil and sauté onion with the rosemary sprigs until onion is translucent. Set aside.

3 Arrange the potato slices, overlapping slightly, in one layer in the baking dish and season with salt and pepper. Cover the potatoes with some of the sautéed onion. Repeat with potatoes, seasoning, and onions.

4 Pour half and half over potatoes, until it just covers the potato slices.

5 Bake for about 45 minutes or until potatoes are soft and top is golden brown.

Scalloped potatoes are pure comfort food. The addition of onion and rosemary is a welcome combination.

Yukon Gold mashed potatoes

Serving Size: 4

6	medium Yukon Gold potatoes, quartered	6
2	cloves garlic, halved (optional)	2
¼ cup	butter	50 ml
½ cup	milk	125 ml
	salt and pepper to taste	

1 Boil the potatoes and garlic in salted water until tender when pierced with a knife.
2 Drain the potatoes and garlic and place in a stand-up mixer with a paddle attachment, or simply break up potatoes with a masher.
3 Add butter, milk, salt, and pepper and mash for about 30 seconds. Potatoes should be light and creamy with lumps and skins mixed in.

The garlic in this recipe is not overly pronounced, and adds depth of flavour. Omit the garlic and enjoy the natural buttery flavour of these yellow fleshed potatoes.

Tomato mango avocado salsa

Serving Size: 4

2	medium tomatoes, seeded	2
1	avocado, ripe but firm	1
1	mango, ripe but firm	1
½	small red onion, diced	½
1	lime, juiced	1
3 Tbsp	chopped fresh cilantro	45 ml
	salt and pepper to taste	
1 Tbsp	olive oil, optional	15 ml

1 Dice the seeded tomatoes into ½-inch cubes. Peel and pit the avocado and mango and dice into ½-inch cubes.

2 Combine tomatoes, avocado, mango, and red onion in a small bowl. Add lime juice, cilantro, salt, pepper, and oil. Chill and serve.

This is excellent served with grilled fish or chicken.

Blueberry cheesecake

Serving Size: 12

1½ cups	graham cracker crumbs	375 ml
½ tsp	cinnamon	2.5 ml
⅓ cup	butter, melted	75 ml
3 (8 oz)	pkg cream cheese at room temperature	750 g
1 cup	sugar	250 ml
4	large eggs, beaten	4
1 Tbsp	vanilla extract	15 ml
¾ cup	sour cream	175 ml
1 cup	blueberries	250 ml

1   Preheat oven to 350°F.
2   To make the base, combine cracker crumbs with cinnamon and melted butter. Press the crumbs in the bottom and ½ inch up the sides of a 10-inch springform pan. Bake the base for 10 minutes. Set aside. Reduce oven temperature to 225°F.
3   For the filling, beat cream cheese until fluffy. Beat in sugar, and then add the eggs and vanilla. Beat until mixture is smooth. Finally, stir in the sour cream.
4   Pour the filling into the crumb crust and allow the air bubbles to rise to the top. Scatter the blueberries over the surface of the filling and bake for 20 minutes. Reduce oven temperature to 200°F and continue baking for 2 hours. Turn the oven off and leave the cake undisturbed for 1 hour with the door closed.
5   Remove from the oven and cool on rack. Cover with plastic wrap and refrigerate overnight before slicing.

This is a beautiful, creamy cheesecake that does not crack. It looks impressive too with the fresh blueberries studded on top!

Blackberry shortcake

Shortcakes

2 cups	flour	500 ml
¼ tsp	salt	1 ml
1 Tbsp	baking powder	15 ml
3 Tbsp	sugar	40 ml
4 Tbsp	cold butter	50 ml
1	egg, beaten	1
½ cup	milk	125 ml

Whipped Cream

1 cup	whipping cream	250 ml
1 Tbsp	sugar	15 ml
1 tsp	vanilla extract	5 ml
4 cups	blackberries	1 l
	fresh mint for garnish	

1 Preheat oven to 425°F.

2 Mix the dry shortcake ingredients in a medium bowl. Using a pastry blender or 2 knives, cut in butter until it is the size of large peas. In another small bowl, whisk together egg and milk.

3 Add egg and milk all at once to the dry ingredients. With a fork, lightly combine until large clumps form. Turn mixture out onto floured surface and lightly knead until it comes together.

4 Pat the dough into a ¾-inch thick rectangle. Cut dough into 6 rounds or other shapes with a cookie cutter (I like using a star shape). Bake until golden brown, 12 to 15 minutes, depending on size of shortcakes. Cool on a wire rack.

5 Crush ½ of the berries lightly with a fork and spoon over shortcakes that have been split in half. Spoon the remaining berries over the shortcakes and place a dollop of whipped cream on each. Replace shortcake tops and garnish with fresh mint.

The shortcakes in this recipe are tender and crisp. They would be wonderful with any combination of fresh fruit or simply spread with butter and homemade jam.

Peach apricot galette

Serving Size: 6

Pastry

¼ cup	cornmeal	50 ml
2 cups	flour	500 ml
1 tsp	sugar	5 ml
½ tsp	salt	1 ml
¾ cup + 2 Tbsp	cold butter cut into pieces	200 ml
¾ cup	cold orange juice	175 ml

Filling

2 cups	peeled and sliced peaches and apricots	500 ml
½	lemon, juiced	½
3 Tbsp	sugar	40 ml
1½ Tbsp	cornstarch	20 ml
½ tsp	allspice	2.5 ml
1 Tbsp	butter	15 ml

1   Prepare the galette pastry by combining the cornmeal, flour, sugar, and salt in a food processor bowl or large mixing bowl. Add the chilled butter and cut into the flour using the sharp blade of the food processor or 2 knives until the chunks of butter are the size of large peas.

2   Add the chilled orange juice 1 tablespoon at a time. The moment the dough starts to come together, bring it together and wrap in plastic. Flatten the dough into a disk and chill for at least an hour. You will have enough pastry for two 8-inch galettes.

3   Preheat oven to 450°F with a baking sheet or pizza stone inside.

4   While the dough rests, mix the fruit with the lemon juice, sugar, and cornstarch.

5   Roll out ½ of the galette dough on a lightly floured surface. Take a sheet of parchment paper and lay the rolled pastry on the paper. Place the fruit mixture in the centre of the pastry in a mound, leaving a 2-inch border of pastry. Fold the edges of the pastry around the fruit.

6   Using another inverted baking sheet as a large spatula, transfer the galette, keeping it on the parchment, to the heated baking sheet in the oven. Bake for about 15 minutes and reduce oven temperature to 350°F. Continue baking for another 15 minutes or until deeply golden.

This free-form pie is not too sweet and has a wonderfully light, crisp pastry. The pastry recipe makes enough for 2 small galettes, but the filling is only for one, which allows you to make 2 types of fillings. Experiment with the fruit you use. Plums and apples are another exceptional combination.

Fall
at Marché Atwater

Located minutes from downtown Montreal, Marché Atwater brings the bounty of the rural harvest to the city. Public markets have always figured prominently in Montreal. Older markets, such as Marché Bonsecour, were once at the centre of busy urban life. Packed with wagons, carts, and eventually the modern car, Bonsecour provided a place for farmers to sell their produce and livestock and served as a central gathering place for the community. As industry and communities changed over the years, so did the nature and location of the central market place.

In response to closures of other local markets, Marché Atwater opened its doors in 1933. In those early days the market building, with its tall clock tower, was an impressive landmark on the Lachine Canal. Today Atwater is home to many Québec farmers offering fresh produce at excellent prices alongside artisans and specialty merchants who sell meats, cheeses, fish, baked goods, and more.

Stall after stall of fresh produce line the main market building at Marché Atwater. One of the first things that you notice when walking past these vendors are the perfect rows of wooden baskets, full of meticulously arranged fruits and vegetables. Carrots, green beans, and zucchini all stand tall in baskets lined up side by side, creating colourful patterns that delight the eye. There are stands

brimming with bushels of apples as well as a stall full of different kinds of gourds and pumpkins. The people working behind the tables are friendly and eager to answer questions ranging from what to do with a particular kind of apple to the latest developments in the world of hockey.

Many specialty shops line the market building. At the Fromagerie, you can find all kinds of cheeses, including award-winning unpasteurized artisan cheeses, which are handmade in Quebec. There is a fishmonger, a poultry store, and a wonderful specialty wine store. Inside the long market building there are a number of butchers selling everything from venison to Montreal smoked meat. If you're hungry after looking at all this food, stop by the Boulangerie Premiere Moisson and sample freshly made patés, breads, and pastries.

There is something going on at Marché Atwater throughout the year. The people who run the market work hard to involve the community and create an exciting and entertaining atmosphere.

Fall

What to Look for at Marché Atwater

Fall at Marché Atwater is an exciting season. The air is crisp and the deep, rich colours of the leaves mimic the season's harvest. Vendors' tables are packed with baskets of apples and piled with pumpkins. There are cabbages and cauliflowers, plums and ground cherries. The community looks forward to Thanksgiving and the great pumpkin and squash festival in October.

Winter Squash – Winter squash arrive in the fall. They are called "winter" squash because they have such a long shelf life. Summer squash and winter squash are of the same family; the difference is that winter squash develop a hard rind with sweet, deeply coloured flesh. Squash varieties you will most often encounter at the market include acorn, hubbard, butternut, kabocha, and spaghetti. Each variety is unique in flavour and texture. For instance, acorn squash is excellent baked with a little butter and seasoning, while a kabocha would end up being dry, kabochas are better used in soups where its rich flavour can be fully appreciated. When baked, the flesh of spaghetti squash breaks apart into crunchy light strings, which are wonderful served as a simple side dish. Most winter squash can be cut into chunks and roasted or steamed. Squash is wonderful as a purée or used as a natural bowl for your favourite all-vegetable stuffing – a great vegetarian alternative for Thanksgiving. Look for heavy, dark-skinned squash, with few blemishes and no bruises. Whole winter squash should be stored in a cool place and can be kept for months after harvest.

Cabbage – European cabbages can be divided into three types: green-headed, red–headed, and Savoy. Green and red cabbages are heavy, cannonball-like vegetables with sturdy leaves. They are most often used in crunchy coleslaws but are equally good cooked; braised red cabbage is a classic, and pairs especially well with turkey or grilled sausages. Savoy cabbage is a loosely formed cabbage with beautiful crinkly leaves. A Savoy leaf is not as thick as one from a red or green cabbage, so it takes less time to cook and has a lighter texture and milder flavour. It, too, is nice sliced in salads but it is exceptional when used to wrap fish fillets destined for the steamer.

Turkey – In North America, turkeys are traditionally eaten at Thanksgiving. Increasingly, however, turkey is eaten throughout the year as a healthy alternative to other meats. Rather than buying a whole, often very large, bird, try using ground turkey or turkey in pieces. Free-range birds are also available and offer wonderful flavour and texture when cooked. The most important point to remember when preparing turkey is not to overcook it. If you do, you will end up with dry, stringy, chewy meat. Avoid this by using a meat thermometer and basting regularly.

Pork – Pork is very versatile and inexpensive. Pork tenderloin makes for a quick-cooking roast that can be rubbed with spices or glazed with a sweet marinade. Double-thick pork chops are great grilled and taste even better stuffed with your favourite filling; a well-moistened bread stuffing is further enhanced by the natural juices of the meat. Ground pork balances the flavour of beef in meatballs and savoury meat pies. For a quick dinner, sauté slices of pork loin with some apples and serve with puréed yams. Because pork is a lean meat, it is best cooked very quickly or with liquid. For thick chops and roasts be sure to use a meat thermometer for the best results.

Yams – Orange-fleshed sweet potatoes are commonly referred to as yams (technically they are not true yams). When cooked, they have a dense, moist flesh that is remarkably sweet. Unlike potatoes, yams need time to mature above-ground in order to develop their sweetness. Such required storage makes yams an ideal late fall and winter vegetable. Yams can be baked whole, roasted with other root vegetables, or boiled and puréed. Choose firm, thick, heavy yams, and reject any with black spots or bruising. Yams can spoil quickly, so be sure to store them for a short period of time in a cool, well-ventilated space. Do not refrigerate.

Wild Mushrooms – "Wild" mushrooms are available at many public markets these days. Some are specially cultivated, although others remain impossible to cultivate. Flavour and texture varies among mushroom varieties, so experiment. Oyster mushrooms are fan-shaped and white, yellow, or soft pink. They are slightly chewy and have a mild seafood flavour. Chanterelles are truly wild. A prized fungus, chanterelles have a beautiful apricot-gold colour and are shaped like an upturned umbrella. Because they are wild, their flavour varies – from mild to meaty or sometimes nutty – but they will always be tasty. Shiitake mushrooms are cultivated, but they are often included in the "wild" category. Shiitakes are dense and spongy with a wonderful meaty taste. Discard the stems and roast or grill the tops for a deep rich flavour. All should be firm and plump. Store in a paper bag in the refrigerator and use quickly, as they tend to dry out.

Hazelnuts – Shelling your own hazelnuts and roasting them with a little butter and salt is the ultimate autumnal treat. If you haven't eaten all the hazelnuts you've shelled, keep some in the freezer for future use. Coarsely ground hazelnuts are a welcome addition to crumble topping, muffins, or your favourite cereal.

Pomegranates – The pomegranate was celebrated in Greek mythology, art, and poetry as a symbol of fertility. Today, the sight of a pomegranate in the market is a sure sign that fall has arrived. Pomegranates have a beautifully textured bright red rind, which forms a unique crown on top. Inside are hundreds of jewel-like seeds that are refreshingly tart-sweet. These seeds are great as a garnish for salads, and the juice from the seeds can be reduced to a syrup for use in drinks and sorbets. In the Middle East, prepared pomegranate syrup, or pomegranate molasses, is often used in savoury recipes as well as sweet ones. Look for this product in specialty and Middle Eastern stores.

Cranberries – Fresh cranberries make a striking appearance at the market by early October; just in time for Canadian Thanksgiving. They are available fresh right through until December. No wonder they are such a festive fruit! Unlike other berries, cranberries are pretty tough and require cooking. Their characteristic tart flavour is refreshing in baked goods and in condiments for poultry, pork, and game. Dried cranberries are wonderful used in savoury stuffings. Look for hard, shiny, dark-red berries. Fresh berries will keep for weeks in a plastic bag in the refrigerator. They also freeze very well.

Ground Cherries – Also known as caped gooseberries, these exotic fruits are sold in large baskets at Marché Atwater in the early fall. Ground cherries are curious to look at, as the smooth-skinned, marble-sized orange berry is completely enclosed by a parchment-like cocoon. They look very similar to the red-orange Chinese lantern plant and are, in fact, related to the green tomatillo. But what do you do with them? Cape gooseberries are delicious eaten out of hand, stewed for a compote, or used as an exotic garnish for cakes and tarts. The flavour of a ground cherry is a cross between a strawberry, banana, and tomato. The inside is very juicy with many, many, small edible seeds. Peel back a bit of the papery covering and look for deep-orange fruit that is firm and shiny.

Plums – Whether black, red, purple, or green, plums are a delicious early fall treat. Plump and juicy, they are perfectly sized for snacking. If you're lucky enough to have a prune plum tree, you probably know that these plums make excellent jams and tarts. Look for plums that have a bit of "spring" when pressed gently. Store ripe plums in the refrigerator.

Apples – When I think of fall, I think of apples. The markets are full of them – and Canada has so many varieties to choose from – Paula Red, Wolf River, Empire, Racette, Cortland, Gala, Greening, Mac, Braeburns, Spartans, and Jonagolds, to name a few. Each has its own flavour and texture. In season, most apples are extremely crisp and juicy. Empires and Braeburns are wonderful eaten out of hand, while Greenings, like Granny Smiths, are sour and great for cooking. Cortlands are perfect for pies, as they have great flavour and keep their shape when baked. Macs are the ultimate all-purpose apple, good for sauce, pies, and eating out of hand. Look for unwaxed, firm, crisp apples. Vendors will often provide samples of apples to taste. Store apples in the refrigerator and eat as soon as possible.

Fall

Apple pomegranate cider

Fall vegetable soup with fresh rosemary

Smoky chipotle turkey soup

Linguine with toasted hazelnuts, pancetta,
   and Swiss chard

Rigatoni with chanterelles and spinach
   in a garlic cream

Wild mushroom pasta

Green tomato relish

Curried cabbage stew

Maple-baked acorn squash

Puréed yams with vanilla

Shiitake cranberry stuffing

Pomegranate lamb shanks

Pork tenderloin with ground cherry compote

Turkey pot pie with yams on top

Turkey meatloaf

Hazelnut crisp with apples and pears

Classic pumpkin pie

Jan's cranberry applesauce cookies

Old-fashioned apple butter

Warm plum tarts

Apple pomegranate cider

Serving Size: 4

6 cups	unsweetened apple cider	1.5 l
2 Tbsp	pomegranate syrup	25 ml
1 tsp	whole cloves	5 ml
1 tsp	whole allspice	5 ml
2	large cinnamon sticks	2
1 Tbsp	brown sugar, or to taste	15 ml
1 Tbsp	orange zest	15 ml

1 In a saucepan, combine all ingredients; slowly simmer over medium heat for 10 to 15 minutes. Strain hot cider and serve in mugs with additional cinnamon sticks for garnish.

The longer the cider simmers, the stronger the flavour of the spices.

Fresh pea soup from Spring

Strawberries with honeyed
lemon syrup from Spring

Cedar-baked salmon with
warm green bean salad from Summer

Spaghetti with cherry tomatoes
and arugula from Summer

Jan's cranberry applesauce cookies from Fall

Fall vegetable soup with fresh rosemary

Gaga's cheddar pennies from Winter

Classic macaroni and cheese from Winter

Fall vegetable soup with fresh rosemary

Serving Size: 4

1	large onion, diced	1
1	sprig rosemary	1
2 Tbsp	olive oil	25 ml
1	small rutabaga, peeled, in 1-inch dice	1
½ pound	squash, peeled, in 1-inch dice	250g
2	carrots, chopped	2
8 cups	chicken stock	2 l
1	piece Parmigiano-Reggiano rind	1
1 can (14 oz)	navy beans, rinsed and drained	398 ml
2 cups	kale or swiss chard, roughly chopped	250 ml
1	Roma tomato, roughly chopped	1
2 cups	cooked farfalle pasta	500 ml
	salt and pepper to taste	

1 In a large pot, soften the onion with the rosemary sprig in the olive oil over medium heat for about 5 minutes.

2 Add chopped squash, rutabaga, and carrots. Stir to coat with oil. Add the chicken stock and the Parmigiano-Reggiano rind and simmer gently until the vegetables are tender, about 20 minutes.

3 Add the beans, kale, and tomato to the soup and heat through. Finally, add the cooked pasta and remove the Parmigiano-Reggiano rind. Allow the pasta to heat through. Season to taste with salt and pepper and serve immediately.

You can add just about any vegetable to this soup. The real secret is the Parmigiano-Reggiano rind, which adds a great depth of flavour.

Smoky chipotle turkey soup

Serving Size: 6

2 Tbsp	oil	25 ml
1	large onion, coarsely chopped	1
1	large green pepper, coarsely chopped	1
3	stalks celery, coarsely chopped	3
2	large garlic cloves, minced	2
¾ cup	long-grain rice	175 ml
2	bay leaves	2
¼ tsp	dried thyme	1 ml
⅛ tsp	crushed red peppers	1 ml
	salt and pepper to taste	
4 cups	chicken stock	1 l
28 ounces	whole tomatoes with juice	800 ml
1	chipotle pepper, in adobo sauce	1
1 Tbsp	tomato paste	15 ml
½ pound	spicy Italian sausage, in 1-inch pieces	250 g
2 cups	cooked turkey, roughly chopped	500 ml

1 Heat the oil in a large saucepan. Add the onion, pepper, celery, and garlic and cook over moderately high heat, stirring occasionally, until softened, about 10 minutes.

2 Add the rice, bay leaves, thyme, crushed red pepper, salt, and pepper and stir to coat the rice with oil. Add the stock, tomatoes, chipotle, and tomato paste, breaking up the tomatoes against the side of the pot. Bring to a boil, cover, and cook over moderately low heat until the rice is almost tender, about 15 minutes.

3 Meanwhile, in a medium skillet, cook the sausage over high heat until browned.

4 Add the browned sausage and turkey to the soup and cook until rice is tender.

Chipotle peppers are smoke-dried jalapeno peppers and are most readily available canned in adobe sauce. They are smoky hot so you need very little when cooking with them.

Linguine with toasted hazelnuts, pancetta, and swiss chard

1 pound	linguine	500 g
4 Tbsp	olive oil	50 ml
1	clove garlic	1
1 cup	toasted hazelnuts	250 ml
2	slices pancetta, ⅛-inch thick, diced	2
1 cup	chicken stock	250 ml
2 cups	Swiss chard, roughly chopped	500 ml
¼ cup	grated parmesan	60 ml

1 Cook linguine, according to package directions, in a large pot of well-salted water.

2 Meanwhile, heat the olive oil in a frying pan and fry the chopped pancetta until crisp. Add the garlic and toasted hazelnuts and stir briefly, being careful not to let the garlic burn.

3 Add the stock and scrape up any brown bits from the bottom of the pan. Add the chard to the pan and let wilt. Toss chard mixture with drained linguine and garnish with fresh parmesan.

This is a hearty pasta recipe perfect for a cool fall night.

Rigatoni with chanterelles and spinach in a garlic cream

Serving Size: 4

1 pound	rigatoni or penne	500 g
2 cups	chanterelle mushrooms, whole	500 ml
1 Tbsp	garlic, minced	15 ml
2 Tbsp	butter	25 ml
2 cups	whipping cream	500 ml
½ cup	grated parmesan cheese	125 ml
2 cups	raw spinach leaves	500 ml
¼ cup	chives, chopped	50 ml
	salt and pepper to taste	

1. Boil the pasta in lots of salted water.
2. Meanwhile, in a large frying pan, heat the butter over medium-high heat until frothy. Add the mushrooms and sauté until tender and fragrant, about
5 minutes. Add the minced garlic and let soften for about 1 minute, being careful not to let the garlic brown.
3. Add the cream to the mushrooms and let reduce and thicken slightly, about 2 or 3 minutes. Stir in the cheese and then add the spinach leaves. Turn the leaves in the sauce so that they wilt but retain their emerald colour.
4. Finally, add the chives and season with salt and pepper to taste.
5. Add the drained pasta to the skillet and toss with the sauce to warm through. Serve immediately with extra parmesan cheese and ground pepper.

This dish is so yummy it's worth every bit of cream!

Wild mushroom pasta

Serving Size: 4

1 pound	pasta	500 g
¼ cup	butter	50 ml
4 cups	chopped oyster mushrooms	1 l
	salt and pepper to taste	
¼ cup	white wine	50 ml
2 Tbsp	parsley, finely chopped	25 ml

1   While pasta is cooking in lots of salted water, melt butter in a frying pan on medium-high heat.

2   Add mushrooms in small batches, seasoning with pinches of salt and a few grinds of the pepper mill. Once the mushrooms are browned nicely, add a splash of the wine to deglaze the pan, scraping up any browned bits with a wooden spoon. Take off the heat and reserve browned mushrooms in a warm dish and continue with the next batch.

3   Add chopped parsley to the sautéed mushrooms and serve over pasta with freshly grated parmesan cheese.

You can use any variety of mushroom for this recipe. Cremini mushrooms or chanterelles work very well. Be sure to cook mushrooms in small batches so that they brown nicely.

Green tomato relish

3 pounds	chopped green tomatoes	1.5 kg
1 ½ pounds	onions, chopped	.75 kg
2 Tbsp	coarse salt	25 ml
1 ½ cups	white vinegar	375 ml
1 cup	granulated sugar	250 ml
3 Tbsp	pickling spices tied in cheesecloth	45 ml

1 In a large bowl, alternate layers of tomatoes and onions, sprinkling each layer with salt. Let stand 8 hours or overnight. Rinse well and drain well.

2 Combine the tomatoes and onions with the vinegar, sugar, and spices in a pot and bring to a boil. Simmer, uncovered, for 30–45 minutes, stirring frequently.

3 Pour into sterilized jars. Makes about 6 cups or 1.5 l of relish.

This is the classic accompaniment for tourtière, the French-Canadian meat pie (see page 142). It's a perfect recipe for using up all those green tomatoes left on the vine at the end of September.

Curried cabbage stew

Serving Size: 4

2 Tbsp	oil	25 ml
1	large onion	1
1 tsp	garlic, minced	5 ml
1 tsp	ginger, fresh and chopped	5 ml
1 tsp	tumeric	5 ml
½ tsp	mustard seed	2.5 ml
1 tsp	cumin	5 ml
½ tsp	cayenne	2.5 ml
	salt and pepper to taste	
½ cup	crushed tomato	125 ml
¼ cup	water	50 ml
4 cups	cabbage, sliced fine	1 l
1	red pepper, sliced	1
1	yellow pepper, sliced	1
2 Tbsps	cilantro, chopped	25 ml
1 cup	raisins	250 ml
4	lime wedges as garnish	4
½ cup	yogurt as garnish	125 ml

1 In a medium frying pan, heat oil and sauté onion for about 5 minutes or until golden and translucent. Add garlic and ginger. Stir to combine and cook for about 1 minute or until garlic becomes fragrant.

2 Add tumeric, mustard seed, cumin, cayenne, salt, and pepper to the onion mixture and stir to combine. Cook for about 1 minute.

3 Add crushed tomato, water, and finely sliced cabbage to the pan. Stir to combine, cover, and cook for 3 to 5 minutes.

4 Add red and yellow peppers, cilantro, and raisins. Stir and simmer for a few more minutes or until all vegetables are tender-crisp.

5 Garnish with lime wedges and yogurt.

This delectable curried cabbage can be served as a side dish or a vegetarian main course along with basmati rice or couscous.

Maple-baked acorn squash

2	medium acorn squash, seeded and quartered	2
4 Tbsp	butter, melted	50 ml
8 Tbsp	maple syrup	125 ml
	sprigs fresh thyme for garnish	

1 Preheat oven to 375°F.
2 Arrange squash quarters, skin side down, on a foil-lined baking tray.
3 Drizzle with butter and syrup.
4 Bake for about 30 minutes or until tender. Garnish with fresh sprigs of thyme.

Acorn squash is the perfect match for maple syrup. It couldn't be easier to prepare and makes an elegant side dish.

Puréed yams with vanilla

2	large yams, peeled	2
¼ cup	butter	50 ml
½ cup	milk	125 ml
½ tsp	pure vanilla extract	2.5 ml
	salt and pepper to taste	

1 Chop the yams into large chunks and boil in salted water until tender, about 20 minutes.

2 Drain the yams and add the butter and milk. Beat with an electric hand mixer until smooth. Stir in the vanilla and season to taste with salt. Keep warm until ready to serve.

> **Inspired by Mark's Place in Fort Lauderdale, Florida, the vanilla in this recipe balances the sweetness of the yams perfectly. This purée is wonderful served with Pomegranate lamb shanks (see page 100).**

Shiitake cranberry stuffing

Serving Size: 6

3 Tbsp	butter	40 ml
2	large onions, diced	2
2 cups	chopped celery	500 ml
1	sprig fresh rosemary	1
1 pound	shiitake mushrooms caps, chopped	1 l
1 Tbsp	oil	15 ml
1 pound	seasoned ground pork sausage meat, optional	500 g
2	Granny Smith apples, peeled and roughly diced	2
1 cup	dried cranberries	250 ml
8 cups	stale bread cubes	2 l
¼ cup	chopped parsley	50 ml
1 tsp	dried sage	5 ml
1 tsp	dried thyme	5 ml
	salt and pepper to taste	
1 cup	tawny port wine	250 ml
1 cup	chicken stock	250 ml

1   Heat 1 tablespoon of the butter in a large frying pan. Sauté onion, celery, and rosemary over medium heat until softened, sweet, and fragrant, about 10 minutes. Transfer mixture to a large mixing bowl.

2   Increase the heat to medium high and add chopped mushrooms. Sauté the mushrooms until lightly browned. Add the mushrooms to the mixing bowl.

3   In a little bit of oil, cook the sausage until lightly browned, breaking it up with a spoon as necessary. Drain and add to mushroom mixture.

4 Add the apples, cranberries, breadcrumbs, herbs, salt, and pepper to the vegetable mixture. Toss lightly. Add the port and stock and toss until well moistened.

5 Place the stuffing into an 18–20 pound turkey. If you choose to bake the stuffing by itself, bake in an ovenproof dish at 350°F, covered, for approximately 30 minutes.

This stuffing matches well with poultry, pork, or even acorn squash.

Pomegranate lamb shanks

Serving Size: 4

4- ¾ lb	lamb shanks	4- 375 g
2 Tbsp	oil	25 ml
1	large onion, roughly chopped	1
4	large carrots, roughly chopped	4
5	cloves garlic, minced	5
1	bay leaf	1
1 cup	red wine	250 ml
2 cups	chicken stock	500 ml
1 can (28 oz)	whole tomatoes, drained	796 ml
1 cup	tomato juice, reserved from can	250 ml
¼ cup	pomegranate syrup	50 ml
	water to cover shanks	
½ cup	fresh pomegranate seeds	125 ml
½ cup	chopped parsley	125 ml

1 Preheat oven to 350°F.
2 Season the shanks with salt and pepper and brown in a large, heavy pot with an ovenproof lid. Remove shanks and reduce heat. In the same pot, sauté onions until soft and golden. Add carrots and stir in garlic.
3 Add the wine, scraping up the browned bits from the bottom of the pan. Add chicken stock, tomatoes, juice, and pomegranate syrup.
4 Return shanks to the liquid and add enough water to cover the bones.
5 Bring to a boil, cover, and place in preheated oven. Cook for 2 hours.
6 Garnish with pomegranate seeds and chopped parsley.

Unlike grenadine, pomegranate syrup is dark and thick as molasses. It is available at specialty stores and Middle Eastern markets. This dish is excellent with puréed yams with vanilla (see page 97).

Pork tenderloin with ground cherry compote

4 cups	ground cherries, skinned	1 l
½ cup	sugar	125 ml
1 cup	water	250 ml
½ tsp	allspice	2.5 ml
	salt and pepper to taste	
2 pounds	pork tenderloin	1 kg
1 Tbsp	oil	15 ml

1   Combine the fruit, sugar, and water in a saucepan. Cook over high heat for about 15 minutes or until fruit is soft enough to mash.

2   Add allspice, salt, and pepper. Let cool. Add oil to half of compote.

3   Preheat oven to 400°F.

4   Season tenderloin with salt and pepper. In a medium roasting pan on the stovetop, brown the meat over high heat.

5   Remove the pan from the heat and spread compote over pork loin.

6   Bake 25 to 30 minutes or until meat thermometer registers 160°F. Let meat rest for 2 to 3 minutes before carving.

7   Serve with remaining compote.

Turkey pot pie with yams on top

Pastry

2 cups	flour	500 ml
¾ tsp	salt	3 ml
¾ cup	shortening	175 ml
¼ cup	butter	50 ml
¼ cup	cold orange juice	50 ml

Filling

4 cups	chicken stock	1 l
1	stalk celery	1
1	bay leaf	1
4	sprigs thyme	4
1	large carrot, peeled and in 1-inch pieces	1
½ pound	raw turkey breast, cut into 1-inch pieces	250 g
2 cups	chopped red new potatoes	500 ml
1 cup	peas, fresh or frozen	250 ml
5 Tbsp	butter	75 ml
1	onion, diced	1
6 Tbsp	flour	75 ml
½ cup	half and half	125 ml
¼ cup	chopped parsley	50 ml
2	yams, peeled and quartered	2
1 Tbsp	butter	15 ml
¼ cup	milk	50 ml
	salt and pepper to taste	

1 Prepare pastry by combining the flour and salt in a food processor bowl or large mixing bowl. Add the chilled butter and shortening and cut into the flour using the sharp blade of the food processor or 2 knives until the chunks of butter are the size of large peas. Add the orange juice

1 tablespoon at a time. The moment the dough starts to come together, stop working it and wrap it in plastic. Flatten the dough into a disk and chill it for at least an hour.

2   In a medium saucepan heat the chicken stock with the celery, bay leaf, and thyme. Bring to a boil and then reduce to a simmer. Cook the chopped carrots in the stock for about 2 minutes until tender crisp. Remove from the stock with a slotted spoon and reserve. Poach the turkey pieces until cooked through, about 3 to 4 minutes, and reserve, and then parboil the potatoes for about 2–3 minutes. Finally, blanch the peas until bright in colour. Remove the celery and thyme sprig; discard.

3   In another medium saucepan, melt the butter. Add the diced onions and sauté until softened and slightly browned. Remove from the heat and stir in flour to form a paste. Return to the heat and let cook for 30 seconds. Using a whisk, add the reserved warm chicken stock a bit at a time. Once smooth, continue stirring and bring to a boil, being careful to scrape into the corners of the pot. The sauce should be thickened at this point. Add the half and half and bring back to a simmer. The sauce is ready when it thickly coats the back of a spoon. Stir in chopped parsley.

4   Drain any liquid that has collected in the plate of the reserved vegetables. Add the vegetables and turkey to the sauce and combine.

5   Meanwhile, boil the chopped yams until tender. Drain and mash with butter, milk, salt, and pepper. Reserve.

6   Line a deep pie plate with pastry and blind bake for 15 minutes at 450ºF. Remove from the oven and pour in the pot pie mixture. Cover with spoonfuls of pureed yams. Reduce oven temperature to 375ºF and bake pot pie for 35 to 40 minutes. Let cool slightly before serving.

A classic cozy fall dish that's worth the effort!

Turkey meat loaf

2 Tbsp	olive oil	25 ml
3 cups	chopped yellow onion	750 ml
1½ tsp	salt	7.5 ml
1 tsp	thyme leaves or ½ tsp dried	5 ml
⅓ cup	Worcestershire sauce	75 ml
¾ cup	chicken stock	175 ml
1½ tsp	tomato paste	7.5 ml
5 pounds	ground turkey breast	2 kg
1½ cups	plain breadcrumbs	375 ml
3	extra large eggs, beaten	3
¾ cup	ketchup	175 ml

1 Preheat oven to 325°F.

2 In a frying pan, heat the olive oil and add onion, thyme, salt, pepper. Cook over medium-low heat until onions are translucent, about 15 minutes. Add the Worcestershire sauce, stock, and tomato paste. Mix well. Let cool to room temperature.

3 Combine turkey, breadcrumbs, eggs, and onion mixture. Mix well and shape into a rectangular loaf on a parchment-lined baking sheet. Place a pan of hot water in the oven below the meat loaf, which will keep the top from cracking. Spread the ketchup over top of meat loaf and bake for 1½ hours, until the internal temperature reaches 160°F.

This is the ultimate comfort food and great served with mashed potatoes and braised red cabbage. This is a large recipe so expect some leftovers for sandwiches.

Hazelnut crisp with apples and pears

Serving Size: 6

½ cup	flour	125 ml
¼ cup	whole hazelnuts, toasted	50 ml
¼ cup	oats	50 ml
3 Tbsp	sugar	45 ml
6 Tbsp	butter	75 ml
4 cups	apples and pears, peeled and sliced	1 l
¼ cup	brown sugar	50 ml
½ tsp	cinnamon	2.5 ml
½	lemon, juiced	½

1   Preheat oven to 350°F.
2   Using a food processor or a sharp knife, finely chop toasted hazelnuts. Combine with flour, oats, and sugar in a medium-sized bowl. Using your fingers, work the butter into the flour mixture until it resembles coarse meal. Reserve the topping in the fridge.
3   In a deep pie plate or baking dish, combine the prepared fruit with the sugar, cinnamon, and lemon juice.
4   Crumble the topping over the fruit. Bake for 40 to 45 minutes or until golden and bubbly around the edges.

The toasted hazelnuts add a nice crunch to this crumble.

Classic pumpkin pie

Pastry

1 cup	flour	250 ml
½ cup	shortening	125 ml
½ tsp	salt	2.5 ml
3–4 Tbsp	cold orange juice	45–60 ml

Filling

1 can (14 oz)	pumpkin puree	398 ml
1 tsp	ground cinnamon	5 ml
½ tsp	ground nutmeg	2.5 ml
½ tsp	ground ginger	2.5 ml
½ tsp	salt	2.5 ml
1	pinch ground cloves	1
1 can (13.5 oz)	evaporated milk	385 ml
½ cup	sugar	125 ml
1	egg, lightly beaten	1
2 Tbsp	molasses	25 ml
1	9-inch pie crust, unbaked	1

1 Prepare pastry by combining the flour and salt in a food processor bowl or large mixing bowl. Add the chilled butter and shortening and cut into the flour using the sharp blade of the food processor or 2 knives until the chunks of butter are the size of large peas. Add the orange juice 1 tablespoon at a time. The moment the dough starts to come together, stop working it and wrap it in plastic. Flatten the dough into a disk and chill it for at least an hour.

2   Preheat oven to 450°F.

3   Roll out pastry on a lightly floured surface and line a 9-inch pie plate. Chill.

4   Beat together all ingredients. Pour into the pie shell and bake for 20 minutes. Reduce heat to 350°F and continue baking for 25 to 30 minutes or until centre is just set but jiggles slightly.

Using canned pumpkin for this pie is not only easy but makes for a silky-smooth consistency.

Jan's cranberry applesauce cookies

Serving Size: 2 dozen

2 ½ cups	12-grain bread mix	625 ml
	(available at bulk food stores)	
3 cups	oats	750 ml
1 cup	golden raisins	250 ml
1 cup	dried cranberries	250 ml
1 ½ tsp	baking powder	7.5 ml
1 tsp	salt	5 ml
½ tsp	nutmeg	2.5 ml
¾ cup	butter, softened	175 ml
2 cups	brown sugar, packed	500 ml
2	eggs	2
¾ cup	unsweetened applesauce	175 ml
1 ½ tsp	vanilla	7.5 ml

1   Preheat oven to 325°F
2   Combine bread mix, oats, raisins, cranberries, baking powder, salt, and nutmeg in a medium bowl.
3   In a large bowl, cream the butter and sugar until light and fluffy. Beat in eggs, one at a time, and then add the applesauce and vanilla.
4   Add the dry ingredients to the butter mixture and stir until well combined.
5   Drop cookie dough onto ungreased cookie sheet using a tablespoon. Bake for 18 to 20 minutes or until nicely browned. Let cool on sheet for about 5 minutes and then remove to a rack and let cool completely before storing.

These are very moist cookies and the addition of dried cranberries adds a nice tang.

Old-fashioned apple butter

Serving size: 4 cups

4 pounds	apples, washed, cored, and cut	2 kg
2 cups	water	500 ml
½ cup	brown sugar	125 ml
1 tsp	cinnamon	5 ml
½ tsp	ground cloves	2.5 ml
¼ tsp	ground allspice	1 ml
1	lemon, juice and grated zest	1

1 In a large pot, combine the apples and water. Cook slowly until soft.
2 Pass the fruit through a fine strainer and for each cup of fruit pulp, add the sugar, spices, lemon juice, and zest.
3 Cook the fruit over low heat, stirring constantly until the sugar is dissolved. Continue to cook, stirring often, until the mixture coats the back of a spoon and has no liquid separating from it when a spoonful is put on a plate.
4 Pour into hot sterilized jars and seal or store in the fridge for up to 1 month or freeze for longer storage.

Use Wolf River apples or Macs for this delicious apple butter. Spread the butter on buttered toast or use as a condiment for roasted pork and poultry.

Warm plum tarts

Serving Size: 6

1	package frozen puff pastry, defrosted as per package instructions	1
6	plums, pitted and thinly sliced	6
6 Tbsp	sugar	75 ml
½ tsp	cinnamon	2.5 ml
1 Tbsp	unsalted butter, cut into small pieces	15 ml
2 Tbsp	apricot jam, heated, optional	25 ml

1 Preheat oven to 375°F.
2 Roll out pastry to a thickness of ⅛ inch on a lightly floured surface. Cut out six 5-inch rounds and transfer to a parchment-lined baking sheet.
3 Overlap plum slices on top of pastry rounds, leaving a ¼-inch border of pastry showing.
4 Mix sugar and cinnamon together and sprinkle evenly over plums and dot with butter.
5 Bake in the middle of the oven for about 25 minutes or until puffed and golden brown.
6 Transfer tarts to a cooling rack. Brush the tarts lightly with the warm apricot jam to glaze. Serve warm with ice cream.

This is a quick and easy dessert for entertaining.

Winter
at St. Lawrence Market

The St. Lawrence Public Market has a long history as the central market for Toronto. My grandmother remembers going to the market with her family on the weekend. Back then, there were farmers selling not only fruits and vegetables but also livestock. Although livestock is no longer for sale at the St. Lawrence, farmers still gather and sell their meat and produce just as they have been doing for over 75 years.

Located downtown, the St. Lawrence Market provides Toronto with a historical and agricultural focus. The market comprises a North and South Market building; the South Market building was once Toronto's original City Hall and dates back to 1845. Many renovations later, the large stone building remains and is now a permanent home to a variety of meat, cheese, and produce vendors. The North Market building, located directly across the street, is the present-day site for the local farmers' market, which is held every Saturday.

As you step inside the South Market entrance, you notice the echo created by the high ceilings. It is dimly lit and there is usually a saxophonist busking in one of the corners. Inside the main space, the market comes alive. There are cheeses – everything from Ontario cheddar to huge wheels of imported Parmigiano-Reggiano – stacked so high that you can barely see the people behind the counter. Then there are the butchers, and there are many at the St.

Lawrence. Not only do they sell classics such as peameal bacon but also special-ty meats such as ostrich, veal, and pheasant. If all this food makes you hungry, line up for a peameal bacon sandwich at the Carousel Bakery.

In the basement of the South Market you'll find all sorts of spices and grains, as well as a few deli and food counters. Up on the second floor, the City of Toronto Archives has a standing exhibit of photographs of old Toronto.

Across the street, at the North Market, over 50 Ontario growers gather to sell their produce. The tradition of the Saturday market started in 1803, and some shoppers arrive as early as 5 a.m. to buy the freshest food in town. The North Market is filled with table after table of massive cauliflowers, with all their leaves intact, bunches of kale, and artisan breads and cheeses. If you're at the North Market on a Sunday, you'll have a chance to check out the antique market. Whether it's hosting a Christmas festival or the starting point for a 10-kilometre race through the city, St. Lawrence Market remains a centre for fresh food and activity all year long.

Winter

What to Look for at St. Lawrence Market

There's a foot of snow outside and the cold stings your face, but step inside the St. Lawrence Public Market and you will find the butchers, bakers, and cheese shops bustling with business. Handmade signs clutter the cheese stalls advertising everything from huge blocks of Ontario cheddar to locally produced feta. Meat vendors display racks of ribs and countless cuts of beef, poultry, pork, and game.

Parsnips – Cream-coloured parsnips are sweet during late fall and throughout the winter months. Their rich, nutty flavour is especially good mixed into mashed potatoes. Parsnips are related to carrots and have a similar appearance. Unlike carrots, however, the central core of parsnips can be woody and should be trimmed away. Choose parsnips that are firm. Store in the refrigerator in an open plastic bag.

Sharp Cheddar – Sharp Ontario Cheddar is glorious. Its flavour is deep and rich and its texture firm but slightly crumbly. Requiring up to seven years of aging, it is available throughout the year but seems to suit winter recipes best. Cheddar can be used in savoury biscuits, quiche, and soufflés. Serve a chunk with apples or, better yet, as the gooey basis for a grilled cheese sandwich.

Kale – Kale is a welcome winter green that is full of vitamins and minerals and holds up beautifully when cooked. Its blue-green leaves are sturdy with tightly curled edges. Due to its toughness, kale must be cooked, but even after 10 to 15 minutes of simmering or sautéing it retains its texture and bright emerald colour. Kale is a wonderful addition to winter vegetable soups or simply sautéed with olive oil and garlic. Look for bunches of kale that are stiff and crisp without any signs of yellowing. Keep in a closed plastic bag in the crisper of the refrigerator for a week or more.

Onions – Just about everyone has onions in the house, and why not? Onions are the basis for most cooking. Storage onions have had their outer skins dried and, if kept in a cool, dry space, will keep for months at a time. When cooked slowly and allowed to turn soft and translucent, onions become sweet and tender. Although most appreciated for their flavouring in a recipe, onions can stand alone in a caramelized onion tart or as the main ingredient for a curry or pizza. Look for onions that are hard and heavy for their size. Pass over any that give when squeezed or have black blemishes.

Grains – From rice to quinoa, grains are the perfect staple for winter cooking; they store very well in airtight containers and are rich in nutrients and protein. They can be used as the basis for salads or soups or play a supporting role, complementing other hearty foods. Grains add a nutty, chewy texture to a recipe and can often be interchangeable; just be sure that the cooking times are similar. A grain like quinoa, for example, which doesn't require soaking or a lengthy cooking time, is wonderful when used to thicken a vegetarian chili. Grains include barley, bulgar, quinoa, and wheat berries. Don't forget the wide variety of rice as well – basmati, jasmine, wild rice, short grain, long grain, brown, even Thai red rice – to add texture and taste.

Pulses – Dried beans, lentils, and peas are another important winter ingredient. They can be cooked and puréed, or used whole in soups, stews, chilis, and salads. Most beans and peas require soaking overnight and about 35 to 40 minutes of simmering, depending on their age and size. Once cooked, beans should be tender but not mushy. A smaller pulse, like red lentils, can be added directly to a stew or curry without being soaked.

Spices – Spices liven up the winter palette not only with their heat but also with their colour and fragrance. Imagine the smokiness of chipotle peppers, the deep amber colour of a curry, or the gentle scent of nutmeg baking in the oven. Consider spices as ingredients to play with. Experiment with those you are unfamiliar with. If you want to test out the flavour before fully committing to it, simply take a few spoonfuls of your sauce and add a tiny bit of the spice. This way you can sample the flavour combination without potentially ruining your meal. If you use whole spices, toast them first in a frying pan to enhance the flavour before grinding. Rather than use bottled, pre-ground nutmeg, buy whole nuts and grate them yourself. Store spices in airtight containers and buy only small quantities to guarantee freshness.

Cured Meats – Most butchers have a wide selection of deli meats available, some of which have been salt-cured or air-dried and allowed to mature for months at a time. After months of dry-curing, these cuts of ham or beef have a very dry, hard appearance and should be served sliced transparently thin.

Probably one of the best-known cured hams is Italian prosciutto. However, the German varieties, Westfalian ham and Baurenschinken, are often overlooked. These hams have a wonderfully salty, smoked flavour and are excellent served with crusty bread and grainy mustard. Experiment with the unfamiliar; the butcher may even allow you a taste if you're curious. Well-wrapped dry-cured meats keep up to one week in the refrigerator.

Peameal Bacon – Peameal bacon is a salt-and-sugar cured unsmoked pork loin that has been rolled in fine cornmeal. This type of bacon originated in Ontario and, in years past, it was rolled in dried pea meal; hence the name. It is a lean bacon with a salty-sweet flavour. It's at its best sliced and simply seared in a pan and served with eggs and toast. The Carousel Bakery at the St. Lawrence Market is famous for its peameal bacon sandwich, and if you want one on a Saturday morning you'll have to line up!

Beef – Although available year-round, beef is hearty enough to be included in the winter category. When you think of beef, don't limit yourself to cuts of steak or prime rib; consider the so-called "lesser" cuts. If cooked properly, flanks, shoulder meat, and neck meat yield tremendous flavour and value. Who can resist a rich goulash or braised beef stew served with crusty warm bread on a cold winter night? These tougher cuts of beef come from the working muscle of the animal so they have lots of connective tissue that, when cooked slowly in liquid, break down and make the meat meltingly tender and full of flavour. Choice cuts of beef are from less-worked muscles, such as the back, and require dry heat, shorter cooking times, and higher temperatures. Marbling, which refers to the streaks of fat in the meat, serves to baste the meat as it cooks. In fact, a great percentage of this fat melts away and in the end is not eaten. So, rather than choose an extra-lean cut of beef, choose one that is well marbled for maximum flavour and tenderness.

Mussels – In general, the colder months are the best time to indulge in a big bowl of steamed mussels. When mussels and other shellfish, such as clams and oysters, spawn in warm water, their energy is depleted and their meat becomes tough and tasteless. When reproduction is complete, mussels can spend their time getting plump.

Look for mussels that have solid shells and are heavy for their size. If some shells are open, press them closed. If they remain closed, they are alive. If a mussel remains open when raw or stays closed when cooked, it is dead and should be discarded.

Winter

Apricot nutmeg scones

Gaga's cheddar pennies

Peameal bacon breakfast strata

Baurenschinken with parmesan scrambled eggs

Peameal bacon sandwich

Classic macaroni and cheese

Rustic wheat berry soup

Coconut saffron shellfish stew

Orecchiette with curried cauliflower and kale

Rosemary-roasted root vegetables

Potato-onion curry with black mustard seeds

Ontario cheddar cheese soufflé

Chipotle pepper chicken

Southwestern chili

Rustic Irish stew

Peppered flank steak with garlic-sautéed kale

Heidi's knödel

Tourtière

Red pepper chutney

Apricot nutmeg scones

Serving Size: 12

2 ½ cups	flour	625 ml
½ cup	sugar	125 ml
1 Tbsp	baking powder	15 ml
1 tsp	baking soda	15 ml
½ tsp	salt	2.5 ml
¼ tsp	nutmeg	1 ml
½ cup	butter	125 ml
¾ cup	half and half	175 ml
1	egg	1
1 tsp	vanilla	5 ml
½ cup	dried apricots, roughly chopped	125 ml
1	orange, grated zest	1

1   Using a pastry blender or 2 knives, mix flour, sugar, baking powder, soda, salt, and nutmeg together in a large bowl. Cut in butter to the size of large peas.
2   Mix half and half, egg, and vanilla together.
3   Mix with dry ingredients until just combined.
4   Mix in chopped apricots and grated zest. Knead mixture briefly on lightly floured surface until dough comes together. Roll out dough about 1 inch thick and cut as desired.
5   Bake at 375°F for 20 minutes on a parchment-lined cookie sheet.

These scones are light and golden and the addition of nutmeg makes them smell – and taste – delicious.

Gaga's cheddar pennies

Serving Size: 6

½ pound	well-aged cheddar, grated	250 g
½ cup	butter, cut into pieces	125 ml
¼ tsp	salt	1 ml
¼ tsp	cayenne	1 ml
1¼ cups	flour	300 ml
¼ cup	water, chilled	50 ml

1 Mix the flour, cheddar, salt, and cayenne together in a bowl.
2 Work in the pieces of butter with your hands until it resembles coarse meal; add the water a little at a time, and bring the dough together gently. Cover and chill for at least 1 hour.
3 Roll the dough to a thickness of ¼ inch and cut into 1¼-inch rounds.
4 Bake at 375°F for about 15 to 20 minutes or until lightly browned and crisp.

These are buttery little cheddar bites that are great with cocktails or just as a savoury snack.

Peameal bacon breakfast strata

½ Tbsp	oil	7 ml
9	slices peameal bacon	9
1	small onion, sliced	1
1	clove garlic, minced	1
4 cups	cubed Italian bread (with crust)	1 l
2 cups	shredded sharp cheddar cheese	500 ml
3	large tomatoes, seeded and thickly sliced	3
2 cups	milk	500 ml
¼ cup	chopped fresh basil	50 ml
	salt and pepper to taste	
¼ tsp	dried thyme	1 ml
6	eggs, lightly beaten	6

1 In a large frying pan heat the oil and sear the bacon until nicely browned. Remove the bacon and reserve. Add the onions to the pan and sauté until soft and translucent. Add the garlic and sauté for 1 minute. Set aside.

2 Preheat oven to 325°F.

3 Arrange 2 cups of the bread cubes in the bottom of a lightly greased 9 x 9-inch baking dish; top with half of the cheese and half of the onion, bacon, and tomato slices.

4 Whisk together the milk, basil, salt, pepper, thyme, and eggs. Pour half of this mixture over the tomatoes. Layer the rest of the ingredients in the same way, reserving a little of the cheese to sprinkle on top. Cover and chill for at least 1 hour or up to 24 hours.

5 Bake, uncovered, at 325°F for 45 to 55 minutes or until the strata is puffed and golden. Let stand for 5 minutes before serving.

Bauerenschinken with parmesan scrambled eggs

Serving Size: 4

3 oz	Baurenschinken, sliced paper thin	100 g
4	English muffins, toasted	4
6	large eggs	6
	salt and pepper to taste	
½ Tbsp	butter	7 ml
¼ cup	parmesan (Parmigiano-Reggiano preferred), finely grated	50 ml

1 Beat the eggs and season with salt and pepper. In a medium, non-stick pan, scramble the eggs over medium-high heat for 3 to 5 minutes. Remove the pan from the heat once the eggs have set but are still very wet.

2 Stir in the grated cheese. The eggs will continue to cook due to the residual heat of the pan and should become beautifully creamy.

3 Divide the sliced Baurenschinken among one half of the English muffins and place the scrambled eggs on top. Cover with the English muffin tops.

Bauerenschinken is smoked, dry-cured pork; prepared and served like proscuitto but with a light, smoky flavour.

Peameal bacon sandwich

Serving Size: 1

3	slices peameal bacon	3
1	large sourdough kaiser roll	1
1	fried egg (optional)	1

1 In a skillet, brown the slices of bacon over high heat. Remove from pan and reserve.

2 In the same pan, over medium-high heat, crack the egg and fry until the white is opaque.

3 Place the bacon and egg inside the fresh roll and enjoy!

Inspired by the classic at St. Lawrence's Carousel Bakery.

Classic macaroni & cheese

Serving Size: 6

5½ cups	milk	1.4 l
6 Tbsp	butter	75 ml
½ cup	flour	125 ml
	salt and pepper to taste	
½ tsp	nutmeg	2.5 ml
pinch	cayenne pepper	
4½ cups	sharp cheddar cheese	1 l
2 cups	gruyere cheese	500 ml
1 pound	elbow macaroni	500 g

1   Heat oven to 375°F. Heat milk and set aside.
2   Melt 3 tablespoons of butter in a saucepan. Add flour and cook, stirring for 1 minute. Whisk in hot milk until smooth and continue stirring over medium-high heat until thickened. Sauce should thickly coat the back of a wooden spoon.
3   Remove from heat and add spices and ¾ of the cheese. Set aside.
4   In plenty of boiling water, cook pasta 2 to 3 minutes less than package directions. Rinse and drain completely. Stir macaroni into cheese sauce and pour into a large buttered baking dish. Sprinkle with remaining cheese.
5   Bake until browned on top and sauce is bubbly; about 30 minutes.

Try different shapes of dried pasta, such as penne and cavatappi, if you like. In you want to add some crunch, melt 2 tablespoons of butter and mix with 1 cup of fresh breadcrumbs. Sprinkle over top of macaroni and bake as directed.

Rustic wheat berry soup

Serving Size: 8

1 cup	dried white navy beans	250 ml
1 cup	wheat berries	250 ml
2 Tbsp	olive oil	25 ml
1	onion, roughly chopped	1
4	cloves garlic, minced	4
1 Tbsp	chopped fresh sage	15 ml
1 Tbsp	chopped fresh rosemary	15 ml
1 can (14 oz)	diced tomatoes, with juice	398 ml
3 cups	chicken stock	750 ml
3 cups	water	750 ml
½	small head of cabbage, halved, cored, and coarsely chopped	½
2	carrots, chopped	2
½ pound	green beans, cut in ½-inch lengths	250 g
¼ cup	chopped fresh parsley	50 ml
	salt and pepper to taste	

1   Soak dried beans and wheat berries separately, in enough water to cover, for 8 hours or overnight.

2   Drain the wheat berries and reserve. Drain the beans and place in a large pot; add cold water to cover by about 1 inch. Bring the water to a simmer and cook, slightly covered, for about 45 minutes to 1 hour or until beans are tender but still hold their shape. Do not drain. Set aside to cool.

3   Meanwhile, in a large pot, heat oil and add onion. Sauté until softened. Add garlic, sage, and rosemary. Cook until fragrant. Add wheat berries, tomatoes, stock, and water to the pot and bring back to a simmer.

4   Cover the pot and cook until the wheat berries are tender, about 1 to 1½ hours.

5 Add cabbage, carrots, green beans, and reserved navy beans with their liquid. Bring to a simmer and cook until vegetables are tender, about 25 minutes.

6 Stir in parsley and season with salt and pepper.

This soup is full of hearty winter vegetables. Serve with lots of crusty bread.

Coconut saffron shellfish stew

Serving Size: 4

2 cups	chicken stock	500 ml
1	shallot, minced	1
2	cloves garlic, sliced	2
1 tsp	fresh ginger, minced	5 ml
1	pinch saffron threads	1 ml
1 tsp	chili peppers	5 ml
4	kaffir lime leaves	4
1	stalk lemongrass, white part only, cut into 1-inch pieces	1
½	lime, juiced	½
1 Tbsp	tomato paste	15 ml
1 cup	coconut milk	250 ml
1	red pepper, thinly sliced	1
1	yellow pepper, thinly sliced	1
1 pound	tiger prawns, peeled, deveined	500 g
1 pound	clams	500 g
1 pound	mussels, cleaned and debearded	500 g
¼ cup	chopped parsley	50 ml

1 In a large pot, combine chicken stock, shallot, garlic, ginger, saffron, chili peppers, kaffir lime leaves, lemongrass, and lime juice. Boil for 3 to 4 minutes.

2 Stir in tomato paste and then the coconut milk. Simmer for about 5 minutes.

3 Add the clams and mussels to the simmering coconut milk mixture and cover, giving the pot a shake to evenly distribute the shellfish. Cook for 3 minutes and then add the prawns and peppers. Cover the pot and shake again. Continue to simmer until the shellfish have opened and the prawns are pink, approximately 2 to 3 minutes.

4 Sprinkle the stew with the chopped parsley and serve.

Shellfish is a welcome treat in the winter, breaking the monotony of winter meat dishes. Serve this stew with small bowls of steamed rice.

Orecchiette with curried cauliflower and kale

Serving Size: 4

1 pound	orecchiette	500 g
2	medium onions, thinly sliced	2
1 Tbsp	olive oil	15 ml
	salt and pepper to taste	2.5 ml
½ Tbsp	curry powder	7 ml
1½ cups	chicken stock	375 ml
2 cups	chopped cauliflower, in 1-inch pieces	500 ml
1	small bunch kale, roughly chopped	1

1 In a large pot of salted water, cook pasta according to package directions. Drain and reserve.

2 Meanwhile, in a large pan, sauté onion with the salt and pepper, in oil over medium-low heat for 15 to 20 minutes. Onions should be caramel-coloured and soft.

3 Stir in curry powder and add chicken stock. Bring to a simmer.

4 Add cauliflower and kale and cover. Cook for 10 minutes or until vegetables are tender.

5 Toss with cooked pasta and serve immediately.

"Orecchiette" means little ears. Their shape is perfect for holding onto sauces with pieces of vegetables.

Rosemary-roasted root vegetables

Serving Size: 6

4	Yukon Gold potatoes	4
4	large parsnips, peeled	4
4	large carrots, peeled	4
4 Tbsp	olive oil	50 ml
4	sprigs fresh rosemary	4
	salt and pepper to taste	

1 Preheat oven to 400°F.
2 Cut the potatoes and parsnips into long wedges, and the carrots in half lengthwise.
3 Place in a baking dish, add the cut carrots, and drizzle with olive oil. Add the rosemary sprigs and season with salt and pepper.
4 Roast, uncovered, for about 20 to 30 minutes or until vegetables are tender.

Roasting root vegetables intensifies their natural sweetness with the added bonus of crisp edges and beautiful colour.

Potato-onion curry with black mustard seeds

Serving Size: 4

2 Tbsp	oil	25 ml
2	medium onions, finely sliced	2
1 tsp	tumeric	5 ml
1 tsp	cumin	5 ml
	salt and pepper to taste	
½ tsp	cayenne pepper	2.5 ml
1 tsp	black mustard seeds	5 ml
3	large potatoes, peeled and chopped	3
1 can (28 oz)	diced tomatoes, with juice	796 ml
1	bunch spinach, stems removed	1
¼ cup	cilantro, chopped	50 ml

1   Heat oil in a deep frying pan or medium pot. Add sliced onion and sauté until translucent and golden brown.

2   Add tumeric, cumin, salt, pepper, cayenne, and mustard seeds and combine with onions. Fry the spices for a minute to release their flavour.

3   Add diced raw potatoes and stir. Then add the crushed tomatoes and enough water to the pan so that the liquid completely covers the potatoes. Allow curry to simmer, covered, for about 30 to 40 minutes or until potatoes are quite soft. At this point the oil should have separated and will be floating on the surface of the curry.

4   Just before you are ready to serve, add the spinach leaves and stir into the curry so that they will wilt but retain their colour. Garnish with chopped cilantro and yogurt.

This is a great curry to make when your cupboards are bare. Serve with basmati rice.

Ontario cheddar cheese soufflé

Serving Size: 4

4 Tbsp	butter	50 ml
4 Tbsp	flour	50 ml
1⅓ cup	milk, heated	300 ml
½ tsp	salt	2.5 ml
1	pinch cayenne	1
½ tsp	dijon mustard	2.5 ml
1⅓ cup	aged cheddar cheese, grated	150 ml
4	egg yolks, well beaten	4
4	egg whites	4
½ tsp	cream of tartar	2.5 ml

1 Preheat oven to 350°F.
2 Wrap a strip of folded aluminum foil around a 2-quart (2-litre) soufflé dish, forming a 2-inch (5-cm) collar. Set aside.
3 On medium heat, melt butter in a saucepan until foamy. Add flour and stir with a wooden spoon to form a paste. Keep stirring and let cook for about 30 seconds.
4 Add hot milk, salt, cayenne, and mustard to the roux and whisk until slightly thickened. Mixture should coat the back of a spoon.
5 Take the white sauce off the heat and stir in grated cheese. Whisk in egg yolks.
6 In a clean bowl, using clean, dry beaters, whip egg whites, adding cream of tartar when the whites are foamy. Beat whites until they form stiff peaks.
7 Gently fold egg whites into the cheese sauce until just blended. Do not overmix.
8 Pour mixture into the prepared soufflé dish. Place a baking dish into the preheated oven and, with a measuring cup, pour water into the pan about halfway up the edge. Place the soufflé dish in the pan of water and bake for about 45 to 50 minutes or until the top is set and nicely browned.

Chipotle pepper chicken

Serving Size: 6

6	legs chicken, split in half	6
	salt and pepper to taste	
3 Tbsp	olive oil	45 ml
2	onions, chopped	2
3	cloves garlic, minced	3
2 cups	chicken stock	500 ml
2 cans (28 oz)	whole tomatoes, drained	1.5 l
2	whole chipotle peppers, seeded and chopped	2
4 cups	nugget potatoes, halved	1 l
2 Tbsp	adobe sauce (from the chipotle can)	25 ml
1	red pepper, sliced	1
1	yellow pepper, sliced	1
¼ cup	parsley, finely chopped	50 ml
6	lime wedges	6

1. Pat the chicken pieces dry and season well with salt and pepper. Heat olive oil in a large frying pan and brown chicken pieces. Remove from pan and set aside.
2. Sauté onions in the oil remaining in the pan until soft and golden. Add garlic and stir to combine. Add nugget potatoes and stir to coat with onion mixture. Cook for 1 to 2 minutes.
3. Add chicken stock and canned tomatoes, scraping up brown bits from the bottom of the pan. Stir in the chopped chipotle peppers and the adobe sauce. Bring the mixture to a simmer and add the reserved chicken pieces. Cover the pan and simmer slowly over low heat for about 30 minutes.

4 When the chicken legs are cooked through remove them from the pan and reserve. Increase the heat to high and reduce the cooking liquid until it is slightly thickened and the potatoes are tender. Reduce heat to low.

5 Add the sliced peppers to the sauce and sprinkle with half of the parsley. Return the chicken to the sauce to warm through. Garnish with the rest of the parsley and a wedge of lime.

This recipe provides great smoky flavour with a bit of kick. Buy chipotle peppers canned in adobe sauce in the Mexican section of your local grocery store.

Southwestern chili

1 pound	ground pork, optional	500 g
2 Tbsp	oil	25 ml
2	medium onions, chopped	2
6	cloves garlic, chopped	6
2	carrots, chopped	2
1 can (28 oz)	diced tomatoes, with juice	796 ml
1 can (14 oz)	kidney beans, rinsed and drained	398 ml
1 can (14 oz)	black beans, rinsed and drained	398 ml
½ tsp	sugar	2.5 ml
1	bay leaf	1
½ tsp	crushed red pepper, or to taste	2.5 ml
1	red pepper, seeded and chopped	1
1 cup	frozen corn	250 ml
	salt and pepper to taste	
¼ cup	chopped fresh parsley	50 ml

1 In a large pot, heat the oil and brown the ground pork.
2 Reduce the heat to medium low. Add the onions and sauté for about 20 minutes or until golden and very soft. Add the garlic and carrots and cook for 2 to 3 minutes.
3 Add the tomatoes, beans, sugar, bay leaf, and crushed red pepper to the pot. Stir to combine and bring to a boil. Reduce to a low simmer and add the red pepper and corn. Cook for 20 to 30 minutes or until thickened slightly. Season to taste.
4 Stir in chopped parsley and serve.

This chili freezes very well and is excellent served over couscous or rice.

Rustic Irish stew

Serving Size: 4

2 Tbsp	oil	25 ml
3 pounds	lamb shoulder pieces, bone in	1.5 kg
1	large onion, sliced	1
3	garlic cloves	3
3	sprigs fresh rosemary	3
4 cups	chicken or beef stock	1 l
2	tomatoes, chopped	2
12	nugget potatoes, whole	12
6	large carrots, cut into large chunks	6
½ cup	pearl barley	125 ml
	salt and pepper to taste	
¼ cup	chopped fresh parsley	50 ml

1 In a large heavy pot, heat the oil over high heat. Sear the lamb pieces until dark brown on all sides. Remove meat and reserve. Reduce the heat to medium and sauté the onions, rosemary, and whole garlic until the onions are golden and translucent.

2 Return the meat to the pot and add the stock, chopped tomatoes, and potatoes. (If you are using chunks of cut potatoes, add them about 40 minutes before the end of the cooking time.)

3 Bring to a boil, then simmer slowly, uncovered, for about 1 hour. Add the carrots and the pearl barley and cook until meat, vegetables, and barley are tender, about 30 minutes.

4 Season with salt and pepper. Stir in chopped parsley and serve. This stew is even better the next day.

This stew is hearty enough to serve all on its own.

Peppered flank steak with garlic-sautéed kale

Serving Size: 4

2 pounds	flank steak	1 kg
	salt and freshly-ground	
	mixed peppercorns to taste	
3 Tbsp	olive oil	40 ml
2	cloves garlic, minced	2
1	bunch kale, stems removed	1
½ cup	chicken stock	125 ml

1 Rub steak on both sides, with 2 tablespoons of the oil. Season flank steak generously with salt and pepper. Let stand for 20 to 30 minutes.

2 Grill the steak for about 2 to 3 minutes per side or until medium rare. Let rest briefly, then slice thinly across the grain.

3 Heat 1 tablespoon of oil in a medium-sized frying pan. Add the garlic and the kale. Toss to coat with oil and allow the kale to wilt. Add the chicken stock and continue to cook until most of the liquid has evaporated and the kale is tender-crisp.

This is a nice wintertime bistro-style meal, and is excellent served with mashed potatoes.

Heidi's knödel

1	large onion, diced	1
3 cups	soaked and drained white bread	750 ml
2 pounds	ground meat (mixture of beef and pork)	1 kg
¼ cup	capers, drained	50 ml
	salt and pepper to taste	
2 Tbsp	herb seasoning salt	25 ml
2	large eggs, lightly beaten	2
2 Tbsp	oil	25 ml
¼ cup	chopped parsley	50 ml
3 cups	chicken stock	750 ml
1 pound	fettuccine or rotini pasta	500 g

1 Soak leftover stale bread in water and then squeeze out by hand. Break it up well until it resembles lumpy oatmeal.
2 Combine the meat, capers, salt, pepper, seasoning salt, and eggs in a large bowl and mix well. Form the meat into 1-inch balls.
3 In a large, heavy frying pan (a well-seasoned cast iron pan is perfect for this), brown the meatballs in batches in the oil. It is important to let them go dark and crispy, as this will flavour the broth that follows.
4 Once the meatballs are browned, drain off excess fat and add the chicken stock to the pan. Bring to a boil and then reduce the heat to medium-low, cover, and let simmer for about 15 to 20 minutes.
5 Cook pasta according to package directions. Drain and serve with meat-balls and plenty of broth. Garnish with chopped parsley.

These German meatballs are exceptionally light and moist.

Tourtière

1 Tbsp	vegetable oil	15 ml
2 lb	ground pork	1 kg
1½ cups	beef stock	375 ml
3	onions, finely chopped	3
3	cloves garlic, minced	3
1 cup	finely chopped celery	250 ml
	salt and pepper to taste	
½ tsp	each cinnamon, pepper, savory	2.5 ml
¼ tsp	ground cloves	1 ml
1 cup	dried breadcrumbs	250 ml
½ cup	chopped fresh parsley	125 ml

Pastry

¾ cup	vegetable shortening	175 ml
¼ cup	butter	50 ml
2 cups	flour	500 ml
¾ tsp	salt	3 ml
¼ cup	cold water	50 ml

1 In a large frying pan, heat the oil over medium-high heat; cook pork and beef, breaking it up with wooden spoon, until no longer pink. Drain off fat.

2 Stir in stock, onions, garlic, celery, salt, cinnamon, pepper, savory, and cloves. Bring to a boil. Reduce heat to medium and simmer, stirring occasionally, for 35 to 45 minutes or until about 2 tablespoons of liquid remains.

3 Remove from heat and stir in breadcrumbs and parsley. Taste and adjust seasoning. Cover and refrigerate until cold.

4 Prepare pastry by combining the flour and salt in a food processor bowl or large mixing bowl. Add the chilled butter and shortening and cut into the flour using the sharp blade of the food processor or 2 knives until the

chunks of butter are the size of large peas. Add the water 1 tablespoon at a time. The moment the dough starts to come together, stop working it and wrap it in plastic. Flatten the dough into a disk and chill it for at least an hour.

5   Preheat oven to 375°F.

6   Roll out pastry for the bottom crust and line a 9-inch pie plate. Roll out pastry for the top crust and reserve.

7   Spoon pork mixture into pie shell, smoothing out the top. Cover with pastry and flute pastry edges. Decorate with extra pastry as desired. Cut steam vents into top pastry and bake for 40 to 45 minutes or until golden brown. Cool for about 10 minutes before serving. This pie also freezes very well. Serve with red pepper chutney or green tomato relish.

This classic French-Canadian spiced meat pie is traditionally served on New Year's Eve after midnight mass. Serve with red pepper chutney (recipe follows).

Red pepper chutney

Serving Size: 3 cups

4 cups	chopped tomato	1 l
1 cup	chopped onion	250 ml
¾ cup	chopped green pepper	175 ml
¼ cup	chopped red pepper	50 ml
¼ cup	chopped celery	50 ml
¼ tsp	crushed chili peppers	1 ml
¾ cups	white vinegar	175 ml
¾ cups	granulated sugar	175 ml
	salt and pepper to taste	
½ tsp	nutmeg, allspice, cinnamon, cloves, ginger, and celery seed	2.5 ml

1 Place everything into a large, heavy saucepan and bring to a boil.
2 Reduce heat and simmer, uncovered, about 2½ hours, stirring frequently until thickened.
3 Serve with tourtière, poultry, or pork.

This recipe makes enough for one tourtière plus a little extra.

Index